BLOODY BRITISH
HISTORY

BURY ST EDMUNDS

C000273328

BLOODY BRITISH HISTORY

HISTORY

BURY ST EDMUNDS

ROBERT LEADER

The
History
Press

The History Press
The Mill, Brimscombe Port
Stroud, Gloucestershire, GL5 2QG
www.thehistorypress.co.uk

British Library Cataloguing in Publication Data.
A catalogue record for this book is available from the British Library.

ISBN 978 0 7524 6287 5

Typesetting and origination by The History Press
Printed in Great Britain

CONTENTS

INTRODUCTION

AHA, CAUGHT YOU!

Having a quick preview, were you?

Well, if you're looking for a serious history of Bury St Edmunds, put this book down immediately. Go away. This book is not for you.

On the other hand, if you're looking for a quick, fascinating read, a racy narrative that just takes in the bloody and the brutal bits, all that's gory, ghoulish and bizarre, then this could be just the book you're looking for!

This is a shortened history with all the boring bits snipped out. It won't tell you when the railways came, or when the Town Hall was built, or how many tons of sugar beet were processed in the year whatever.

None of that. It's just the battles and the beheadings, the hauntings and the hangings, the witchcraft and scandals and the murders. Its Bury laid bare, Bury in the raw, Bury warts and all. So be warned...

AD 500

THE SLAUGHTERED SAINT

IN THE BEGINNING, before it was called Bury St Edmunds, this small Saxon settlement on the River Lark was called Beodricksworth.

We can get a glimpse of what early Bury may have looked like by going a little further down the river. At West Stow, archaeologists have excavated and rebuilt the site of one of these small early Saxon settlements. This one had half a dozen thatched huts and was probably home to two or three close families.

They may have originated somewhere in Europe. They may have fled together to escape from the raping and burning prevalent among the warring Germanic tribes, all trying to grab a piece of the action after the collapse of Rome. In this scenario, they would have braved the terrifying North Sea with its cold grey waves and pitiless storms. They would have been wretched, half drowned, shivering and seasick before they found their way into the wide estuary of the Wash. From there they would have made their way up the Great Ouse River, through an alien landscape of misty swamps and marshes. As they turned up the little Ouse and then into the Lark they may have felt more at home as the dark forests closed around them. Finally, they would have found a riverbank clearing and stopped to clear their new settlement.

Alternatively, at Beodricksworth their male leaders may have been mercenaries who had fought for Rome, veterans of years of hard frontier warfare before the Empire had withdrawn. Before the collapse, it was Roman policy to reward its soldiers with small pieces of land in retirement.

Either way, West Stow and Beodricksworth took shape. Both settlements would have been surrounded by a nightmare world of untamed forest, the haunt of ravening wolves and wild boar. The wolves hunted in packs and would have been capable of tearing to pieces and devouring a small child, the

Saxon Arms.

ABOVE *Saxon arms and armour.*

TOP *The Saxon village at West Stow.*

weak and the crippled. The boar would have been savage, snorting terrors with sharp tusks, fatal to any hunter or traveller who slipped and fell in their path. The early Saxons only had bows and arrows, swords and spears for hunting, and to defend themselves. Their lives would have been short, fearful and hard.

In the sixth century, the great Saxon King Raedwald became the King of all East Anglia. He was succeeded by a son name Erpwald, who was soon murdered, and then by another son named Sigbercht. The latter built a small monastery at Beodricksworth between the River Linnet and the River Lark and briefly retired there as a monk. He had renounced his crown to his son, Egric. A Mercian army invaded East Anglia and Sigbercht abandoned his prayers to go and help his beleaguered son. It was a bad move, and Sigbercht met a bloody end in battle.

It was against this background of warring Saxon Kingdoms that the Vikings decided that they would cut themselves in for a bit of raping and plundering. There was not much to do in Scandinavia, and they were all good sailors in their sturdy longships. There were plenty of Christian monasteries springing up around the British Isles at this time, so if the local women were not too tasty they could always grab a few ecclesiastical treasures as a consolation prize.

Cue the arrival of King Edmund, who became King of East Anglia in the middle of the sixth century. The first pirate attacks of the Vikings had, by now, swelled into a full-scale invasion by a Danish Army, which had been terrorising the whole of eastern England for the past thirteen years. The Danes had got into the habit of making their winter camp near Thetford and, somewhere nearby, Edmund challenged them in a final bloody battle.

Sadly, Edmund lost. The Danes butchered the Saxons with their broadswords and battle axes, and those that were not chopped down on the field fled for their lives. Edmund ran with the rest, but somehow got separated from all his friends. According to one version of the story, he ended up at Hoxne, by the River Waveny.

The boy King must have been terrified and exhausted. The Danes had slaughtered the bulk of his army and his friends, and chased him until he could run no further. In desperation, he sought a hiding place and tried to conceal himself under a bridge that spanned a little side-stream of the river.

He was out of luck. A bridal party chose to cross the bridge while he was hiding underneath. They saw the silver glitter of Edmund's spurs reflected in the water, and leaned over for a closer look – and in so doing betrayed his position to the pursuing Danes.

The Vikings hauled him out and tied him to an oak tree. The Vikings were pagans and Edmund was a Christian. They had fun at his expense, offering to spare his life if he would renounce this new God. Edmund refused. So they whipped him until the blood ran. Still he refused to deny Christ, and so they

Stone roundel depicting St Edmund hiding under
Goldbrook Bridge.

started to use him for target practise and shot him full of arrows. When they tired of that sport – and by this time he was said to be bristling like a hedgehog with all the feathered shafts that had pierced his body – they hacked off his head. It was a savage and brutal end.

Goldbrook Bridge at Hoxne is said to be modelled on the original bridge where Edmund took refuge. An oak tree was later found nearby with arrow heads still embedded in the trunk; a small obelisk in a farmer's field now marks the spot.

The story continues with Edmund's followers searching for his body. They kept calling his name as they stumbled through the woods. In answer, a disembodied voice kept calling, 'Here, here, here.'

Eventually the searchers found the headless corpse. Nearby, in a bramble thicket, they discovered the severed head. According to the legend, the head was being guarded by a ferocious she wolf who sat with the head between her paws. Edmund's lips were moving and it was the head that had been calling, 'Here, here, here.'

The martyrdom of St Edmund:
a stained glass window in St Mary's church.

Goldbrook Bridge, where St Edmund hid
from the Danes.

THE VIKINGS

The Vikings rose in the ninth century to become a formidable power on land and sea. From their homelands in Scandinavia, they penetrated as far south as the Bosphorus and eastward into the Russian steppes, following the great natural river routes of Europe. For more than 100 years their dreaded longships terrorised the Saxon shores of England, and twice full-scale armies of the Norsemen invaded East Anglia.

The first raids on the Kent coast were reported in AD 789, and in AD 793 the Vikings looted the great monastery at Lindisfarne in Northumbria. Their long, narrow ships, powered by oars and a large square sail, were ideal for penetrating rivers and estuaries and made the perfect vehicle for lightning attacks in search of loot and plunder.

As they had quickly learned at Lindisfarne, the churches and monasteries were the richest targets for their raids. The holy buildings were filled with sacred treasures, golden crosses, silver chalices, gem-studded bibles and golden plates and goblets. By just stripping the altar alone they could more than pay for the cost of the voyage. And shrines were only defended by unarmed monks – or even better, by a nice plump flock of nuns. It was no wonder that the Vikings kept coming.

Viking fleets crossed the wild North Sea and thrust into Ireland and Northern England. In AD 865 it was the turn of East Anglia, and the Scandinavian Great Army overran both counties.

After the defeat and death of Edmund it was left to another English King, Alfred the Great, King of Wessex, to finally halt this first invasion of the Danes. In AD 878 Alfred won a major battle at Edington in Wiltshire and forced a treaty on their leader, Guthrum. The Danes were too numerous to be driven back over the North Sea, but the treaty limited their expansion to Norfolk, Suffolk and Essex. These were the counties where 'the Dane Law' prevailed.

The Dane Law lasted well into the next century. The rich soils of Norfolk and Suffolk were a vast improvement on their wild and barren homelands and so many of the men who came as pirates and soldiers of fortune stayed as settlers and farmers, and their families and friends came to join them. Gradually they were assimilated into the local Saxon communities.

However, those early Viking raiders were particularly savage characters. They were pagans who worshipped the old Norse Gods. One of their most gruesome practises was the blood-eagle sacrifice, made to honour their god Odin. A captured King or chieftain would have his rib cage hacked slowly open. His lungs would be torn out and draped around his shoulders to create the image of an eagle with folded and blood-dripping wings.

Perhaps St Edmund was lucky that they only shot him full of arrows before they chopped off his head.

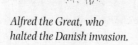

Alfred the Great, who halted the Danish invasion.

Vikings come to Bury! The massacre of Christian priests by the Danes.

The wolf seemed to recognise that her task was over and that these were Edmund's friends. She got up and slowly slunk away.

The head was placed with the body, and miraculously the two parts of the corpse joined together again. The arrow wounds all sealed and healed. A small chapel was built to house the body where it was found, but after thirty-three years it was moved to Beodricksworth and enshrined in Sigbercht's monastery. By this time the remains had become credited with miraculous powers. The corpse had not rotted or decayed in any way and was said to look perfect, as though the young King was merely asleep. The monastery grew into the great Abbey of the town that we now know as Bury St Edmunds, the burial place of St Edmund.

The brutally murdered King was now revered as a saint and a martyr and his shrine grew in size and importance. Around AD 945 another King Edmund, Edmund I of the House of Wessex, granted a large area of land to the growing monastery.

The ravaging Danes were still causing trouble with repeated invasions and demands for their Danegeld, the tribute in gold which they were now extracting from the local earls and Kings. Around 1010 another Danish Army invaded

An obelisk at Hoxne marks the spot where
St Edmund is believed to have been killed.

A bronze statue of St Edmund now
stands in the Abbey gardens – but where
are the saint's bones?

East Anglia and sacked and looted Ipswich and Thetford (among other places). The guardian of Edmund's shrine at the time was named Alwyne and he took the remains of the saint and fled with them to London, where he believed they would be safe.

Old accounts say that the journey was studded with miracles – and with some of the first examples of what became known as 'St Edmund's curse'. An Essex priest who refused to help Alwyne en route had his house mysteriously burnt down. Later, when they arrived in London, an unbelieving Dane who mocked the idea of Edmund as a saint was inexplicably struck blind.

Aldwyne eventually brought his precious charge back to Bury St Edmunds and reinstalled the coffin in the monastery. Then we must assume he was surprised by the return of the Danes, who suddenly appeared again under their King, Sven Forkbeard.

Sven besieged Bury St Edmunds with his army, demanding his Danegold and all the treasures of the church, and threatening to destroy the church and kill all the clergy if he did not get his way. He sat on his warhorse, waving his sword, threatening and blustering, and apparently he tempted fate with some very contemptuous words about the dead saint. Suddenly he saw a vision: in the sky above, riding through the clouds, he saw the dead St Edmund on a ghostly horse, wearing a crown and aiming a silver lance at his heart. Sven was heard screaming that Edmund was coming to kill him and begging his troops for protection. He was then struck dead with an apoplectic heart attack.

Sven's son Canute was present at the siege and watched his father die in convulsions. The incident was sufficiently disturbing to require some heavy thinking. Canute called off the impending attack and went home to gather more reinforcements. He came back with an even bigger army and conquered all of England, becoming King of an Empire which stretched from Bristol to Murmansk.

However, King Canute now knew better than to mess around with Bury St Edmunds, and he knew he needed to make some big atonement for the sins of his forefathers. So he converted to Christianity and rebuilt the Abbey there. He made a pilgrimage to the Abbey and made a gift of his own crown upon the altar. However, he was shrewd enough to buy it back with more gifts of land and an extensive charter of liberties. To make sure that the Abbey was properly looked after from here on, he also replaced the secular priests with twenty Benedictine monks.

Sigbercht's original small monastery was now a Benedictine Abbey and destined to become one of the five greatest Abbeys in England.

The first Abbot of the new Abbey was named Uvius, and it seems that he had the good sense to do his job and leave the saint alone. By this time the saint's curse and his unholy reputation for defending himself was well known. A sheriff who had tried to arrest a woman who had taken refuge

THE ENGLISH WOLF

The grey wolf was once the premier predator of the thickly forested British Isles and Northern Europe. These powerful, savage ancestors of our modern dogs could hunt singly or in pairs, but predominately in packs. A wolf pack would consist of a dominant mating pair, their cubs and perhaps a few subordinate adopted strangers. They hunted by isolating smaller, younger and weaker herd animals, or by tiring larger animals with a long chase until their prey collapsed, exhausted. With the former they would leap for the throat and with the latter they would tear lumps of flesh from the flanks as it ran until the animal bled to death.

The howl of a wolf was a blood-curding sound, more than enough to terrify a lone herdsman or traveller. Wolves communicated by howling, to call the pack together for a hunt, to sound an alarm when danger threatened, or to locate each other in storms, mist or unfamiliar terrain.

The story of a she wolf finding and guarding the head of St Edmund is not unusual, for wolves feature often in medieval myth and folklore. A wolf is said to have suckled Romulus and Remus, the founders of Rome. Wolves feature as gods in Norse mythology and in other cultures wolves have variously been revered as the spirits of ancestors or dead brothers and companions. The ancient Greeks and Romans associated the wolf with the Sun God Apollo.

Wolves have been seen as disguised witches, the creations of an evil spirit, creatures sometimes to be worshipped and sometimes to be shunned or feared. The idea of the shape-shifting werewolf, the cursed human being who could take on the shape, form and deadly attributes of the wolf was prevalent in the Middle Ages. The concept has filtered down into the gore-soaked horror movies of today.

In the ninth century there could only be starlight or firelight after the sun had set. The blackness of night could be long and absolute and frightened imaginations could be triggered by every small rustle of sound. Most people, as Christianity spread, believed in God and the Devil. The wolf was the monster of nightmares, but with divine guidance could also be the most powerful protector. The story of a she wolf guarding the decapitated head of a saint was not a difficult one for medieval man to believe.

As the forests were cleared and the human population expanded, wolves were gradually hunted to extinction. The grey wolf disappeared from England sometime around the middle of the fifteenth century, and the last wolf in the British Isles is said to have been shot dead in Scotland in 1743.

King Canute (here meeting Edward Ironside): he laid the crown on his head on the altar of Bury's Abbey.

in the Abbey shrine had been driven mad, and the same justice had been meted out to a warrior who had simply broken the rules by wearing a sword inside the sacred precincts. Madness and blindness seemed to be Edmund's first choice of weapons.

However, the second Abbot was named Leofstan and he wanted to see for himself whether Edmund's body was really perfectly preserved in its coffin. Perhaps he didn't believe in the curse, or assumed that his prestigious position meant that he would come to no harm. Or perhaps he lifted the lid with some trepidation to inspect the saintly remains. Perhaps he wasn't sure what he was looking at, for the story goes that he actually had the temerity to lay his hands upon the King's head and give it a twist to see if it really was re-attached to the King's body. As a punishment, his hands immediately withered. No doubt a bolt of agony accompanied the horrible shrivelling of flesh, and we can only imagine that Abbot Leofstan dropped the lid back into place pretty quickly.

AD 1066

THE GLORY DAYS OF THE ABBEY

LEOFTSAN'S HANDS WERE in such a mess that King Edward the Confessor sent his own physician to Bury St Edmunds to try and heal them. This was a man named Baldwin, a monk of St Denis who came from the great city of Chartres in France. The two must have got on well, for Baldwin not only tended to the Abbot's medical needs but also shared his duties in helping to run the growing monastery. When Leofstan died, Baldwin became the new Abbot.

Baldwin was still in favour with King Edward: the King granted the Abbey a charter to establish its own mint. Baldwin is also credited with planning a modern town on the Roman rectangular grid pattern and establishing the annual town fair and regular markets for butter, corn, beasts and horses. This was when Beodricksworth first came to be known as Bury St Edmunds. There is a story that, around this time, a mute woman from Winchester named Aelfgeth came to the Abbey, seeking a cure for her dumbness. After praying to St Edmund she found herself cured – and, like any good woman with her speech restored, she immediately used the saint's gift to give a well-deserved tongue-lashing to the nearest menfolk, who in this case happened to be the resident monks! It seems that a period of sloth and torpor had insinuated itself into the Abbey and St Edmund's shrine was not receiving its due care. Aelfgeth soon sorted that out.

In 1066, William the Conqueror landed at Hastings. He was lucky, in that Harold, the resident English King, was busy fighting off another of those endless Danish invasions in the north. By the time Harold had force-marched his army back south into Sussex they were all footsore and weary. The English put up a good fight but the French were rested and they had all had plenty of time to get over their sea-sickness from the channel crossing. Harold got an arrow in the eye – and the rest, as they say, is history.

Bury was lucky in that Abbot Baldwin was still the head of the Abbey. Because of Baldwin's French background, the Normans left him pretty much to get on with it. Baldwin was said to be a brilliant administrator and he successfully managed to keep all jurisdiction over the Abbey and its rights and lands. The new sheriffs of Norfolk and Suffolk didn't like this very much and so for the next 400 years Baldwin's successors seem to have been involved in endless lawsuits in order to hang on to these privileges.

Baldwin's next bit of bother was with Bishop Herfast, who wanted to move the seat of the East Anglian Bishopric from Thetford to flourishing Bury St Edmunds. Baldwin didn't want any other churchman muscling in on his territory, so he took himself off to Rome to plead with the Pope. He must have been a smooth talker – or perhaps it was politically expedient for the Vatican – because he managed to persuade Pope Alexander II to take the monks of Bury St Edmunds under the protection of the Holy See, thus forbidding that a Bishop's See could ever be established in Bury. Herfast's successor, Bishop Losinga, eventually gave up the struggle against the determined Abbot and the Bury monks, and went off instead to Norwich to re-seat himself there as Bishop of East Anglia.

Bury was now growing nicely in the pleasant little valley of the River Lark. There were town walls, earthworks and rivers protecting the town on all sides. There were five gates into the town, all them with hostels for pilgrims, and a small chapel to Our Lady.

Norman knights giving thanks to God after victory at Hastings.

Medieval bridges spanned the rivers Linnet and Lark. For good measure, Baldwin rebuilt the Abbey church with fine Barnack stone. In 1095, the body of St Edmund was transferred with much pomp and ceremony into its new shrine.

The next Abbot of note was Abbot Anselm, the seventh Abbot, who accepted his post in 1121. By this time the great Abbey of Bury St Edmunds had achieved international fame as an intellectual and cultural centre. It was famous for the magnificent illustrated manuscripts produced in its scriptorium. Its position as a centre of pilgrimage for all those wishing to worship at the venerated shrine of the saint had helped to accumulate its great wealth.

The main ceremonial approach to the Abbey was down what is now Churchgate Street. Here there was another small chapel, where the priests could control the assemblies of pilgrims and their endless processions to pay their respects. One of them was King Henry I in 1132.

Anselm continued and extended Baldwin's building work on the Abbey, and he also built a new church dedicated to St James in a corner of the Abbey precincts. He had hoped to make the pilgrimage to the shrine of St James at Compostella in Spain. In this ambition he was frustrated, so building his own church to St James was the next best thing. The church has survived the Abbey, and, with a brand-new millennium tower recently attached, it is now St Edmundsbury Cathedral.

Anselm also built St Mary's church and the great Norman tower that now stands at the bottom of Churchgate Street.

The next great Abbot was Abbot Samson. He inherited an Abbey in debt, and not only managed to restore its finances but also helped raise the ransom to free the wandering King Richard, who had got himself locked up in a German prison on his way home from the Crusades. Samson was also the last man who is known to have opened the coffin of St Edmund.

This happened on the eve of the Feast of St Catherine in 1198, following a serious fire that had damaged the shrine. The blaze had started when one of the altar candles toppled over on its seat of accumulated wax. Too much

Sampson's Tower, built by the last man to open St Edmund's coffin.

inflammable rubbish had been stored under the dais, so there was plenty to feed the flames. The monks realised that they had been neglectful and saw the near disaster as Edmund's way of punishing and reproaching them. They feared for the body inside the coffin, and so Samson opened the lid.

This was over 300 years after the saint's head had been hacked off and his body riddled with arrows, and yet the holy body – according to the legend – was still seen to be intact and without decay, with the head united to the body on a small pillow.

It seems the saint was in a better mood on this occasion: either that or his powers had lessened (or Abbot Samson had the good sense to treat the remains with due reverence and respect). Probably the Abbot learned from Leofstan's experience and refrained from the bad manners of actually testing and pulling anything to see if it would come apart. In the event, there was no reaction from the saint: none of the Abbot's body parts withered or fell off, and the coffin was gently re-sealed.

It was during the reign of Samson that the Jews were expelled from Bury St Edmunds. A boy named Robert had been tortured and murdered, and suspicion fell upon the Jews. As money-lenders they automatically generated envy and dislike, and dark rumours circulated, claiming that they gained their wealth through ritual sacrificial murders. Soon after the boy was buried in the Abbey church, a large number of Jews were murdered in the town.

The rest were evicted on a technicality: Samson petitioned the King in 1190 for written permission to expel the Jews because everything within St Edmund's town belonged to St Edmund. Therefore, either the Jews should be 'St Edmund's men' or they should be banished. The result was that the Jews who had survived the murder spree by the mob were rounded up and marched out of the town by men at arms.

The Abbey not only owned most of the manors of Suffolk but also many stretching up into Norfolk and down into Essex. Henry of Essex was one of the Abbey knights who owed duty and allegiance to the saint, but apparently he incurred St Edmund's wrath by his lack of generosity to the Abbey. This brought about another appearance of the martyr's ghost.

Henry became the King's standard bearer and during an ambush on the Welsh border he came to grief. Believing that the King had fallen, he threw down the standard and withdrew. Another knight, Earl Roger of Clare, galloped up, retrieved the standard and went on to rescue Henry II, who was still alive. A third knight, named Robert de Montford, then accused Henry of Essex of cowardice.

Because they were both powerful noblemen, equal in rank and prestige, there was only one way the dispute could be settled: a personal duel. The two fought in the time-honoured fashion, hewing mightily at each other, blunting their swords and denting their shields and armour.

At the height of this deafening struggle, Henry looked over Robert's shoulder and saw the dreadful spectre of St Edmund scowling from the edge of the field. The saint was dressed in his armour, floating in mid-air and making angry and threatening gestures. Henry was convinced that Edmund wanted to see him punished for his meanness and wickedness. He carried on the desperate fight, but he was so shaken that Robert finally cut him to the ground.

Fornham St Martin, a peaceful Suffolk village - and the scene of two bloody battles.

Henry was left for dead and his body was given to the monks of Reading to be taken away for burial. However, he survived and lived to tell his tale, and eventually became a monk at Reading.

The town of Bury St Edmunds and its great Abbey thrived through the Middle Ages, but the rest of Suffolk and the surrounding countryside were not doing so well. The whole of East Anglia was caught up in the bloody conflict between Henry II and Earl Hugh Bigod, and one of the most savage battles of them all was to take place at Fornham Saint Martin, which was just a few miles outside the town walls.

The Bigods were a powerful and unruly line of Norman Barons who had been giving trouble to the Conqueror and his descendents for the past three generations. Hugh decided to support Henry's grandsons in an armed rebellion.

Hugh ruled roughshod over most of Suffolk from his massive castle overlooking the River Waveney at Bungay. He also controlled Walton Castle and the even more formidable castle at Framlingham. Henry grabbed Walton Castle and garrisoned it with his own troops and then set about building another castle at Orford, which was to block off supplies to Framlingham from the sea.

Hugh was understandably miffed about this. He formed an alliance with the Earl of Leicestershire and, with an imported army of Flemish mercenaries, set about waging his rebellion in earnest. He besieged Walton Castle, but it proved too tough a nut to crack. Frustrated, he drew his forces back to Framlingham for a rest and another thinking session, no doubt fortified by tantrums and ale, and then decided to attack the castle at Haughley, which was also held by knights loyal to the King.

Haughley Castle was in central Suffolk, built on top of a high earth mound and protected by a moat, but this time Hugh's forces were successful. They fought their way across the moat and piled brushwood all around the keep. Once the brushwood was set alight, heat, smoke and sparks poured into the castle, choking the defenders and forcing them out into the open. There they were joyfully butchered; most of those who were not killed in the fighting had their throats brutally cut afterwards. Only the senior knights were saved for ransom.

Ralph de Broc, who was the knight commander of the castle, was killed in the fighting, but few tears were shed on his behalf. Ralph was one of the four knights who had recently visited Canterbury Cathedral to murder the archbishop, Thomas Becket. King Henry had expressed a wish to 'be rid of his turbulent priest,' and Ralph and his friends had rushed out to curry some royal favour. They had stabbed Becket to death and left him lying in a pool of his own blood. Now most of the pious Suffolk peasantry felt that Ralph had got what he richly deserved.

Hugh and his allies were on a winning streak, but it was not to last for long. Robert de Beaumont, the Earl of Leicester, had gone personally to Flanders to raise their force of mercenaries. Now he learned that in his absence Henry's forces were besieging Leicester Castle. Robert and Hugh decided that they would march to relieve Robert's home castle – and at the same time effectively split England in two. The

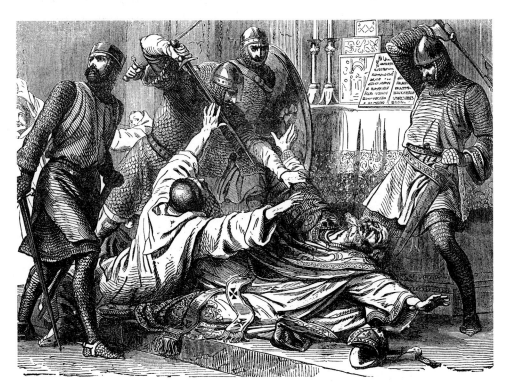

The brutal murder of Thomas Beckett by Ralph de Broc.

23

route of their march passed close to Bury St Edmunds, at Fornham Saint Martin.

Here they came to grief. Henry was absent in France; in fact, his army had just taken another of Leicester's castle's at Breteuil in Normandy. All the Norman lords had lands and holdings in both France and England, so there was a lot of Channel crossing to wage wars on both sides. However, a large army loyal to Henry, under the command of Humphrey de Bohun, who Henry had left as Constable of England, rushed down from the north to intercept the rebels. They were joined by local forces from Bury St Edmunds and under the banner of St Edmund they challenged the rebel army.

It was a massacre. In the marshes bordering the lovely valley of the River Lark it was the turn of the rebels and their mercenary allies to be slaughtered. Humphrey's army smashed them apart – and those that fled were skewered on the pitchforks of the local farmers.

A mercenary army has to live off the land, looting, stealing crops and butchering livestock for food. The Fleming marauders would have been hated for this, and the good yeomen of Suffolk would have had plenty of scores to settle. The river ran red, and blood stained the grassland for miles around. It has been estimated that up to 10,000 Flemings were killed. This was the most savage and bitter battle ever fought in Suffolk and the bodies must have clogged the river for miles downstream. Hugh Bigod fled the field, but the Earl of Leicester and his Countess were captured.

This was the second epic battle to have occurred at Fornham. Previously, in AD 902, the Saxon King Edward, the son of Alfred the Great, successfully fought off a counter claim from a cousin named Aethelwald. Today the whole area is peacefully green and much of it belongs to the Lark Valley Golf Club, but in the later Middle Ages it is not surprising that ploughs were constantly turning up skeletons and skulls, swords, pikes and daggers.

Bury St Edmunds was in the national history books again in 1214. Abbot Samson had died two years previously and the reigning King John was dragging his heels in appointing a successor. It seems that all the revenues due to the Abbey could be appropriated by the King while the Abbacy was vacant, so the monarch had a practical disincentive against speeding up the process. In this case, however, John stabbed himself in the foot – for, with no Abbot to hold any due gratitude to the King for his appointment, the Abbey was wide open to plot and intrigue.

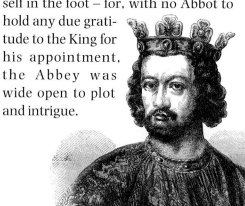

King John.

John was not a popular King, and he had managed to upset most of his Barons by his high-handed manner. He was hated by the general population for his increased taxes, and the monks at Bury St Edmunds were offended by what they saw as his excessive meanness.

John had visited the Abbey in 1119, bringing with him, as was usual in those days, his entire retinue of courtiers and friends. They had cost the Abbey dearly to house and feed them, and on his departure John had contributed a niggardly thirteen pence to the collection plate at the final mass. To add insult to injury, John had even lectured the monks in their own chapter house to remind them of his divine rights when they complained about the need to install a new Abbot.

He finally managed to get himself excommunicated by the Pope. Rome had nominated Stephen Langton as Archbishop of Canterbury, but John had refused to receive Langton in this post. The King wanted to nominate his own man – in his own time, of course – when he had milked Canterbury of as much of its revenues as possible. Pope Innocent III invited the King of France to do the practical job of deposing the King of England.

So King John found himself involved in another war with France. He gathered an army, crossed the channel and hit first by burning Dieppe and destroying all the ships that the French had gathered for an invasion of England. However, at the battle of Bouvines it was the French turn to win a victory and John was forced to return to England.

However, while John was busy fighting in France, his own Barons were secretly uniting behind his back – and the great Abbey at Bury St Edmunds proved the ideal place for them to meet

The Magna Carta and its associations.

John crossing the Wash – narrowly escaping death in the process!

and agree on their plans. Bury was far enough from London to be relatively free of the King's spies. It had no Abbot keeping a high spiritual and moral watch over the behaviour of its monks or their guests, and as a place of pilgrimage it provided the perfect excuse for all of the barons to meet.

They met ostensibly to celebrate St Edmund's day, but their real business was to discuss the Magna Carta, the great charter of human rights that was presented to them by the Archbishop of Canterbury. This was Stephen Langton, the same archbishop that John had tried to reject, but the King's weakening position meant that he finally had to give way.

All the Barons agreed. Twenty-six knights, the most powerful men in England, each swore an oath at the high altar that they would force King John to sign the new charter.

The Barons captured the city of London, which further strengthened their position, and finally caught up with King John in a Sussex meadow at Runymede.

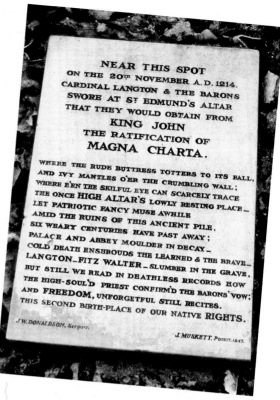

NEAR THIS SPOT
ON THE 20TH NOVEMBER A.D. 1214.
CARDINAL LANGTON & THE BARONS
SWORE AT ST EDMUND'S ALTAR
THAT THEY WOULD OBTAIN FROM
KING JOHN
THE RATIFICATION OF
MAGNA CHARTA.

WHERE THE RUDE BUTTRESS TOTTERS TO ITS FALL,
AND IVY MANTLES O'ER THE CRUMBLING WALL;
WHERE E'EN THE SKILFUL EYE CAN SCARCELY TRACE
THE ONCE HIGH ALTAR'S LOWLY RESTING PLACE —
LET PATRIOTIC FANCY MUSE AWHILE
AMID THE RUINS OF THIS ANCIENT PILE.
SIX WEARY CENTURIES HAVE PAST AWAY;
PALACE AND ABBEY MOULDER IN DECAY —
COLD DEATH ENSHROUDS THE LEARNED & THE BRAVE —
LANGTON — FITZ WALTER — SLUMBER IN THE GRAVE,
BUT STILL WE READ IN DEATHLESS RECORDS HOW
THE HIGH-SOUL'D PRIEST CONFIRM'D THE BARONS' VOW:
AND FREEDOM, UNFORGETFUL STILL RECITES.
THIS SECOND BIRTH-PLACE OF OUR NATIVE RIGHTS.

J.W. DONALDSON, Scripsit.

J. MUSKETT, Posuit. 1847.

John's royal seal on the Magna Carta.

Here the barons swore that they would force King John to sign the Magna Carta.

Runnymead, also known as 'Magna Carta Island', in the early nineteenth century.

27

BROTHER JOCELIN

Jocelin de Brakelond was a monk who lived at Bury St Edmunds' Abbey between 1173 and 1202. Some accounts describe him as the Abbey cellarer, the man in charge of the cellar and stores, and others as a chaplain to Abbot Samson, so perhaps he combined both roles. What is certain is that he kept a detailed chronicle of the life and times of the great Abbey up to the turn of the thirteenth century, and for that all subsequent historians have been eternally grateful.

It is from the Latin writings of Brother Jocelyn that we know so much about the election and the thirty-year rule and administration of Abbot Samson. It is a picture of an Abbot of high integrity and very keen business skills. Under Samson the Abbey prospered and flourished. He inherited an Abbey heavily in debt, but in a few short years he had discharged them all. Samson was obviously held in very high regard in Rome, for he was appointed an arbitrator in various holy disputes: between the Archbishop of Canterbury and the monks of Christchurch; and between the archbishop and the cannons of Lambeth. He was one of three commissioners sent by the Pope to Worcester to investigate the miracles of St Wulfstan.

When Henry II visited the Abbey in 1181, Samson asked for permission to accompany him on the Crusades. He was refused. Later, he was given another commission by the Pope concerning the dispensation of crusaders from their vows and had to journey overseas to consult with the European Kings. He also played a role in collecting the ransom for King Richard and visited the monarch in his German prison.

All of this is detailed in the chronicle of Jocelin de Brakelond, together with all the minutiae of daily life in the great monastery. The monk is described as a cheery and possible cherubic figure, one with a great affection for his Abbot, although an honest monk and not entirely blind to his superior's sometimes high-handed attitude.

The village sign at Fornham St Martin, where Roger Bigod's Flemish mercenaries were massacred.

THE WALK TO ROME

Even before he had become Abbot, the monk Samson had proved himself a man of great courage and determination. The church tithes from the small village of Woolpit, just a few miles from Bury, should have been used to finance the Abbey infirmary. Instead, the money had been misappropriated into the King's coffers. The monk Sampson decided to take this matter into his own hands. So, with a friend, Roger from Ingham, he walked all the way to Rome, a heroic undertaking, wearing only sandals and a robe and with only his staff to aid him. To survive, the two travellers begged for alms. Samson's mission was to obtain a letter from the Pope ordering the King to return the Woolpit monies to the Abbey.

It was a dangerous journey, because at that time there were two rival Popes: Octavian in Avignon, and Alexander in Rome. On the return journey, Samson was attacked by supporters of the French Pope, but they failed to find the letter from the Roman Pope, which Samson hid in his begging cup. Samson eventually succeeded in returning to England, where he presented the Pope's letter to the King. The monarch then had no choice but to return the Woolpit tithes to the Abbey.

There is another strange story linked to the village of Woolpit. Way back in the Middle Ages, two mysterious green-skinned children suddenly appeared from a ditch beside a harvest field in Woolpit. They were a boy and a girl, and appeared to be brother and sister. They spoke a strange language and initially could not explain how or from where they had originated. The perplexed villagers took them to Sir Richard de Calne, the Lord of the Manor. There they were offered food but although they were obviously starved and hungry both children refused to eat until they saw some green beans. They consumed the beans ravenously and for a long time would eat nothing else. The children stayed with Sir Richard. The boy was sick and lethargic and soon died, but the girl grew stronger. Eventually she ate a full diet, and gradually the green pigment to her skin faded. She lived a normal life and was baptised and finally married.

To this day, no one knows where they came from. The girl was eventually able to say that they came from the land of St Martin. Some have interpreted this as Fornham St Martin, the village where the great and bloody battle took place between the forces loyal to King Henry II and the mercenary army hired by the notorious Roger Bigod. If they were the children of Flemish mercenaries or of immigrant workers who had settled in that area, it might explain why they had been forced to flee through the forest and why they spoke an unknown language.

One problem with this theory is the time difference. The children are said to have appeared in the reign of King Stephen, which was before the reign of Henry II and the Fornham battle. Another problem is that the girl also said that the land of St Martin was underground, where the sun never shone and where it was always twilight — and everything was green. There is also that peculiar complication of their skin colour…

John was a King constantly on the move, as he tried to keep one step ahead of his enemies, taking his entire court and his royal baggage trains with him. (He eventually lost his entire treasure trying to cross the Wash when a rising tide caught him midway across – and nearly drowned him with it.)

However, at Runnymede the Barons stood by their oath and forced him to apply his royal seal to the charter. The sixty-two clauses the charter contained were mostly aimed at protecting the feudal rights of Barons and churchmen, but there were two important forward steps: one was that the King should allow justice for every man, and the other that no man should be imprisoned without due legal process.

These were the foundation stones of the British legal system. John refused to sign the charter itself, and the Barons knew that once he had escaped from Runnymede their cunning and deceitful King would try to wriggle out of his promises. So they sent copies of the charter to every cathedral in the land, with the instructions that they must be read aloud every two years.

As the sacred resting place of the remains of King Edmund, Bury St Edmunds had long been renowned as the shrine of a King. Now, as the birthplace of the Magna Carta, it had also become the cradle of the law.

AD 1200

RIOTS AND BEHEADINGS

BY THE THIRTEENTH century, Bury St Edmunds had become a major town and an important agricultural, marketing and commercial centre. As a centre of pilgrimage there were always long processions of footsore and pious visitors paying their respects to the shrine of the saint. These devotees all needed food, drink and accommodation in the inns and taverns. There were dues and contributions to be paid. There was even a Goldsmith's Row, which was a version of a row of modern souvenir shops, selling pilgrim's badges which you could wear to prove you had taken the tour.

These same travellers, for all their prayers and holy purposes, had all the usual human needs – and so the town whores also did a roaring trade. The money poured in.

Abbot Baldwin had kick-started a separate economy by laying out a new street plan and encouraging craftsmen into the town. The weekly markets and the two annual fairs meant more money – and more debauchery. Finally, the flourishing wool trade, which was enriching merchants and landowners throughout Suffolk, brought its benefits and turned Bury into a wool-manufacturing town.

East Anglia had plenty of good grazing land and a good transport system of inland rivers to take cloth and wool to the ports of Ipswich and Norwich; these were only a short channel crossing away from the Continent, where there was an eager market. The soggy fields of Belgium and Northern France had given Continental flocks foot rot, but the dry fields of Suffolk were perfect for the production of the Golden Fleece.

The town was full of spinners, weavers and fullers. The fullers used wooden hammers driven by water mills to pound the raw wool in a mixture of clay and water, which cleaned and thickened it. The spinners turned it into fine skeins on their wooden spinning wheels and the weavers wove

31

the finished cloth. This was a busy medieval town which was also able to support the full range of carpenters and builders, skinners, butchers, bakers, brewers, cordwainers and candle-stick makers who provided for all its needs. A cordwainer, for anyone who has puzzled over the meanings of archaic language and old folk songs, was a shoemaker.

All of this growing prosperity meant that the town burghers were getting fatter and richer – and the aldermen were becoming more aware of their own authority and power. Inevitably, this led to increasing conflict with the primacy of the Abbey. The latter was loathe to part with its tithes and rents and rights, and the former found the twin burdens of cost and submission more and more irksome.

This was still a feudal world, where all power – and most of the land – was divided between the King, his Barons and the Church. In Bury St Edmunds, almost all civic life was controlled by the Abbey and supported by the King's men-at-arms. The discontent of the developing town came to a head in 1293 with some minor riots and the obstruction of the Abbot's bailiffs.

The main causes of debate were who was to elect the town aldermen, who were the town governors or town councillors, and who was to control the five gateways into the town. The townspeople wanted their say and their share and the Abbot wanted to give nothing away. The gate-keepers collected dues and taxes as well as controlling the ebb and flow of people, trade and goods, and so there was much at stake.

A royal commission was set up to resolve the dispute and decided that the town should be allowed to elect its own aldermen unless the Abbot could show some reasonable cause for his objections. It was also decided that the town could elect four of the five gate-keepers. The east gate, which adjoined the Abbot's Bridge, was still to be retained by the Abbey.

This quietened things down for a bit, but failed to relieve all the underlying bitterness between the town and the Abbey. Ten years later there was more violence: the townspeople took up arms again to fight the Abbot's bailiffs, flogging some of the monks (when they were able to catch them), and throwing stones at the workmen trying to repair some damage to the church roof. For all of this the town was fined £200 by King Edward II.

This did not go down well with the aggrieved folk of Bury. They declared war on the monks, and on 15 January 1327 some 3,000 of them stormed the Abbey. They broke down the gates and, despite the screaming resistance of the monks, looted the interior, almost totally destroying the infirmary and the sacristy.

The reigning Abbot at the time was Abbot Richard de Draughton. He was fortunately absent in London when the Abbey was sacked. It was one of his duties to occasionally attend the King's Parliament. When he returned, it was to an unexpected scene of devastation: anarchy, angry townspeople and weeping, infuriated monks.

The townsmen quickly grabbed him and presented him with a charter of

RIGHT *Abbot's Bridge in the
early nineteenth century.*

BELOW *Abbot's
Bridge: this once
stood beside the
busy east gate of
the town.*

liberties they had drawn up in his absence. Just in case Richard had any objections, they had thoughtfully provided a headsman's chopping block and a large, sharp axe, which was placed in full view of these forceful negotiations.

Abbot Richard got the message and, sweating a bit, he hastily applied his seal to the charter with the minimum of argument.

He claimed that he had to go back to London to ratify the charter. As soon as he got there, however, surrounded by the King's soldiers and out of reach of the good burghers of Bury, he promptly repudiated it.

This caused a new wave of rioting to break out in Bury. The monks had by now rallied and armed themselves, and they made a revenge attack on the townsmen while they were at worship in the parish church. All hell was about to break loose. The townsmen collected their sticks and cudgels, farming implements and whatever else was to hand, and retaliated with another attack on the Abbey. This time, after a three-day siege, the entire monastery was all but destroyed.

The Abbey Gate, which had to be completely rebuilt after the riots of 1327.

The Sheriff of Norfolk had to be called in to restore the peace with a strong force of men at arms. This involved hanging many of the leaders of the revolt and declaring as outlaws those they could not find or apprehend. Thirty cartloads of lesser prisoners were dragged off to Norwich to face trial, and a massive fine of £14,000 was imposed upon the town.

Among the list of 300 offenders who eventually faced charges were three rectors and an assortment of merchants, butchers, drapers, tailors and taveners; clearly the whole town was involved. Their crimes included beating and wounding the Abbey servants, fishing the Abbey fish ponds, collecting and stealing the Abbey's tolls and rents, cutting off the Abbey's water supply, and burning down a whole list of the Abbey's manor houses in the surrounding villages.

During the burning spree in the countryside, the rioters had taken care to empty all the barns of corn and to carry away all the Abbey livestock, listed as 100 horses, 120 oxen, 300 bullocks, 200 cows, 10,000 sheep and 300 swine. In besieging the Abbey with armed force and great multitude, they had also broken down all its doors, gates and windows, broken open all its chests and coffers, assaulted the defending monks and looted it of all its gold and silver chalices, books, investments and money to the value of £1,000. The rioters were also charged with taking the Prior and twelve of his monks prisoner, and forcing the Prior to sign various documents and charters they had drawn

up in their favour. Yet more violence was still to come.

Those who had escaped, to become outlaws, managed to kidnap Abbot Richard. They succeeded in smuggling him through London and across the North Sea to Babrant in Belguim. Babrant was then a medieval duchy, one which had also grown rich on the proceeds of the wool trade, so obviously the Bury wool merchants would have had good contacts there. Having already been threatened with the headsman's axe, Abbot Richard must have had a terrifying journey by foot and horseback, and then an equally frightening sea voyage, not knowing what was to become of him. However, his captors only held him hostage until the demand for the £14,000 fine was dropped.

All of this happened in the reign of the recently crowned Edward III, who was busy at the time leading his army in Scotland, trying to reverse the defeat inflicted on his father by Robert the Bruce at Bannockburn. At the end of it all, the Abbey regained all of its original feudal charters; however, it took more than twenty years before the rebuilding work was finished.

The builders and masons had barely taken down the scaffolding from the restored Abbey gateway before the plague struck all of England. In Bury it killed half the population and caused a severe shortage of priests and labourers to work on the monastic lands. This meant that the land workers who

THE BENEDICTINES

The Benedictines followed the rule of St Benedict of Nursia, who founded the first twelve monasteries at Subiaco near Rome in the sixth century when he organised his followers into communities. His rule of life, which incorporated communal living, physical labour, and the distribution of food and alms to the poor, became the model for all the other monastic orders that followed, and revitalised the whole concept of monastic life in central and Western Europe. The order had over 15,000 monks by the end of the fifteenth century, but after the cataclysm of the Reformation less than 5,000 remained.

The great Abbey of St Edmundsbury, at its height, is said to have contained some eighty Benedictine monks — plus the Abbot, some twenty chaplains and over 100 retainers and servants. The Abbot was at the head of the hierarchy, with a Prior in charge of the daily routines within the monastery. The Abbey had a treasurer in charge of all the money; the cellarer would have been in charge of providing food and drink for everybody. The sacrist was responsible for looking after the church, seeing that the candles were lit and the bells were rung. The infirmarer was the monk who ran the hospital and cared for the sick.

Bury's privileged position as a centre of pilgrimage made it not only the largest and most wealthy Abbey in Suffolk, but also one of the five greatest Abbeys in the country. Most of the other religious orders were also represented in Suffolk, but they were all overshadowed by the Benedictines who had seven other Priories, nunneries, and religious houses scattered around the county.

Their daily routine (for those not directly engaged in administration, power politics, and the entertaining of visiting Kings and notables) was one of four to eight hours of prayer and the celebrations of their divine office, from matins at daybreak to vespers and compline at the end of the day. They were allowed seven hours of sleep and, for most of the rank and file, the rest of the time was divided between religious study and necessary work, mainly agricultural, in the gardens and vineyards, or in the fishponds.

A small, talented group would have spent most of their time in the library producing some of the most colourful and brilliantly illustrated Bibles and religious manuscripts in Europe.

Not all of the monks arrived at the monastery gates due to a purely religious calling. In the hungry and poverty-ridden Middle Ages, the life of a monk was, for the poor, one of the few which offered a regular bed, clothing and free meals. They had to work and pray in a world of celibacy and devotion (which was followed with varying degrees of strictness), but they were allowed up to eight pints of beer per day. It was acknowledged that the beer, which the monks brewed themselves, was more fit than water for drinking.

had survived were in a stronger position to press for better conditions and higher wages. Eventually, all these factors, combined with the ill-conceived introduction of a poll tax, caused the Peasant's Revolt.

In 1381, under the smokescreen of this general unrest, the long-suffering people of Bury St Edmunds grabbed the opportunity for another round of rioting and score-settling with the Abbey.

Abbot Richard had passed on, and the Abbacy was again vacant as the current King, this time the young Richard II, vacillated over the next appointment. With no Abbot to vent their wrath upon, the townsmen grabbed a selection of scapegoats: one was the King's Chief Justice, Sir John of Cavendish; another was the Prior of the Abbey, John de Cambridge; the last was the collector of dues, one John of Lakenheath. The latter probably had the ill luck to be collecting the new and much-hated poll tax which the King had inflicted on everyone except beggars.

The Chief Justice and the tax collector had taken refuge in the Abbey, but apparently the frightened monks handed them over to the mob. No doubt they didn't want a full replay of the last riots – but it didn't stop the Abbey from being plundered again. The Prior fled the Abbey, but the rioters caught him at Mildenhall, where he was beheaded.

Cavendish also managed to escape. He got as far as Mildenhall before he was caught and hacked to death. John de Lakenheath was hauled into Bury marketplace, where he had his head chopped off. The headsman's axe lifted and swung before the approving crowd: the blood splashed, and the head rolled.

It was a heady but short-lived victory for the town. Elsewhere, events were moving fast. The Peasant's Rebellion in East Anglia was led by two men named Wat Tyler and Jack Straw. They marched a peasant army upon London and stormed the Tower. There they quickly captured and executed the Lord Treasurer and the Archbishop of Canterbury (with more head-chopping and blood spurting). On the following day they were confronted by the King and some of his knights and ministers at Smithfield. King Richard II was only fourteen years old, so this was quite a brave move.

The rebels were not primarily against the King but against his older ministers, who they saw as cold, hard men manipulating a monarch who was barely more than a boy. They made their demands known: these consisted mainly of the abolishment of serfdom and the removal of the most unpopular of the King's ministers. Wat Tyler is said to have belligerently pushed forward, and was cut down by the Lord Mayor of London, who feared that the boy King was about to attacked.

In the scrum around the King's men, none of the rebels seem to have been fully aware of what had actually happened. The King rode boldly forward and proclaimed that Tyler had been knighted and that they would all meet again at St John's Fields, where all their demands would be met.

It was a lie, but it worked. The mob drew back. The King and his men rode away, presumably taking the body of Wat Tyler with them to maintain the pretence that he was still alive. The ruse gave the King and his knights enough time to organise a small army. The rebels were attacked and Jack Straw and his army were promptly executed in the usual way, their heads cut off and posted high on bloody pikes for all to see.

With London secure and the rebellion (literally) decapitated, the King's government moved again to firmly suppress this new revolt through-out the rest of the country. This was unfortunate for Bury St Edmunds, for retribution against the town for its latest outrage against the Abbey was swift. The town was forced to pay another huge fine – and, when a general national amnesty was declared to allow things to cool down again, Bury was the only town in England to be excluded from it.

No doubt the bitterness and the recriminations must have simmered for a long time afterwards, but Bury seemed to have – at last – learned its lesson. There were no more riots and no more attacks on the Abbey.

THE LAKENHEATH MARKET

Unrest and rioting was not always the result of the long-suffering townsfolk venting their spleen on the Abbey. There was friction between the different ecclesiastical authorities, and it was not unknown for the monks to promote a quarrel. In 1201, it is reported that 600 men marched the 15 miles from Bury to Lakenheath, incited by the monks of the great Abbey, to sack and put an end to a rival market that had been set up there by the Ely monks.

The Prior of the rival St Ethelreda's Abbey in Cambridgeshire had decided to establish the Lakenheath market, no doubt thinking that it was far enough away from Bury for the area to be fair game. Abbot Samson had a different view, and considered the move by the Ely monks to be an infringement of the rights of the Abbey of St Edmund. The Lakenheath market was obviously draw-ing farmers and traders away from the Bury markets, and hence stealing the revenue of taxes and tolls.

The monks at Ely had gained a charter from King John allowing them to hold the Lakenheath market, providing that it did not interfere with neighbouring markets. Samson made a successful petition to the King for the Lakenheath market to be sup-pressed, but this was ignored by the monks of Ely and the market continued. Samson was a tough businessman as well as a pious monk. He sent in his bailiff with a small army of bully boys and orders to arrest the market traders and their customers.

Word of their approach was carried ahead of the raiders, and when they arrived all the traders and farmers had disappeared. The bailiff and his men had to content themselves with tipping over the stalls and breaking up the market goods that had been left behind in the hasty exodus. To compensate for their hike from Bury, they drove off all the cattle and livestock they could find.

One flexing of the Abbey's muscles was enough, and the Lakenheath market was ended.

The monastery church of the Ely monks has survived as Ely Cathedral.

AD 1349–1539

PLAGUE AND FIRE

BURY ST EDMUNDS was hit three times by bubonic plague, the dreaded Black Death that swept repeatedly through the whole of Europe in the Middle Ages. The first wave of fear and horror swept through the town in 1349. It killed off half the population. The streets were littered with corpses, and peasants dropped dead in the fields. No one was spared, not even the monks praying desperately in their great Abbey. It seemed, to the superstitious and ignorant people, as though the grim reaper was sweeping invisibly through the town and countryside, striking mercilessly and indiscriminately with his great scythe.

It was a catastrophe which was to be repeated again in 1589, and then again in 1637.

This terrifying disease originated in the heart of Central Asia and spread with terrifying speed through India, Syria and Asia Minor. It was carried by fleas, which were in turn carried by a plague of black rats. At the siege of Constantinople it was said that infected human corpses were deliberately hurled over the walls to spread the devastating sickness throughout the city and speed its downfall. Once across the Bosphurus, the plague continued to sweep across Europe, killing millions in its path.

In June of 1348 the pestilence reached England. It crossed the English Channel with a fleet of French merchant ships which had sailed from the port of Bordeaux and docked in the Dorset port of Melcombe Regis. The French ships were trading with cargoes of wine, but they were also infested with rats – rats which carried the fleas which carried the plague. Once ashore, the Black Death raced north and infected the whole of England. This was the greatest disaster in the whole history of the British Isles, slashing a population of around five million down to less than three million. Four out of every ten people died.

The unhygienic medieval towns were the ideal places for the disease to take hold and spread, and Bury was no better than the rest. The town was overcrowded, with only crude sanitation and often no washing facilities. The rich could afford half-decent housing, but the living conditions of the poor were usually filthy. The streets had open gutters down the centre where the people threw all their waste. It was not until 1607 that a law was finally passed in Bury St Edmunds forbidding people to allow their pigs to roam in the streets.

The Black Death was characterised by ugly, painful black swellings that would suddenly appear in the neck, groin or armpits of the victim. These would quickly swell and burst, oozing blood. Once a flea had bitten and the disease took hold, very few of its victims survived. The immune system simply collapsed and death was almost always the inevitable outcome. Sufferers did not last long: a few days or a week – and sometimes only hours or minutes. But those final hours or moments were always agonising. It was a particularly cruel and dreadful death.

No one knew the cause of this terrible affliction or how the infection was spread. In this world, there was only one explanation: most people thought that God was punishing them for their sins. The monks in their monastery must have feared that God had at last abandoned them, and that their souls were in as much peril as their bodies.

The combined effects of the Black Death, the Peasant's Rebellion, the beheading of their Prior and the latest sacking of their Abbey must have left the surviving monks demoralised and distraught. Yet still they rallied, and once again began rebuilding the Abbey church, the library and all of the other damaged or destroyed buildings. It must have been heart-breaking work, but what else could they do?

It took the town over five years, in the midst of these troubles, to pay off the fines imposed by the King.

There were, however, continuing plots and intrigues within and without the Abbey. The appointment of an Abbot was a contentious business. It was usually a political appointment made by the reigning King, and confirmed by the Pope in Rome.

This meant that each proposed Abbot had to make the difficult and dangerous journey to Rome to receive the Pope's blessing, and sometimes they did not return. In 1361, Henry of Hunstanton was elected Abbot but died in the plague-stricken province of Avignon while on his way to receive the Papal confirmation. He must have been the first monk of Bury to die from the plague, having the bad luck to meet it half way, before the pestilence had ever reached England.

In addition to the usual tug of war between Pope and King which accompanied most elections, the bishops of Norwich were constantly trying to upset the balance. Ever since their failed takeover of the Abbey in the eleventh century, the Norwich bishops had repeatedly contested the independence granted to the Abbey of St Edmund by

THE HOSPITALS AND THE GREYFRIARS PRIORY

The Abbey had its own infirmary but there were five other medieval hospitals founded in Bury. The most substantial remains today are those of the chapel of St Saviour's Hospital, which stand on Fornham Road behind the modern Tesco supermarket. Saint Saviour's was founded by Abbot Samson in 1148 and was originally intended as an almshouse for the poor, although eventually these recipients were replaced by sick or aged monks.

The Hospital of St Petronilla was a hospital for female lepers which stood outside the south gate of the town. It is the only other hospital from which a clear fragment of the building remains. However, the elegant arch window from St Petronilla's is now on the site of the old Hospital of St Nicholas at the top end of Eastgate Street. After the Dissolution, the St Nicholas site was rebuilt as a private house and it seems that the St Petronilla window was cannibalised into it.

There was a hospital of St John – more usually known as the 'Domus Dei,' or God's House – which was also close to the old south gate.

The ruined window of St Petronilla's hospital now stands on the old St Nicholas hospital site.

The Priory Hotel.

St Stephen's hospital was again in Eastgate Street, and St Peter's was at Out Risbygate. The hospitals were all established on the main roads out of town and provided accommodation to travellers as well as homes to the sick and elderly. They were all founded by different Abbots of the Abbey.

The only other religious house in Bury was the Franciscan Priory founded in 1263 by the Earl of Gloucester in the reign of Henry III. The Franciscans were the Grey Friars who believed that their mission was to take their preaching directing to the people. The Benedictines were, of course, the black monks who remained more aloof and concentrated on their prayers and devotions inside their monasteries.

The Abbey monks were jealous of the Franciscan's role and rule, and the fact that they had papal support. Twice they threw out the Franciscan friars, until finally the Grey Friars abandoned their Priory. The Priory Hotel now stands on the old Priory site on Mildenhall road, close to the Tollgate Public House.

All the medieval hospitals were closed down at the Dissolution.

the Pope. The wealth and power accumulated by the Abbey meant endless rounds of Abbey politics, and these did not exclude the many internal intrigues.

In 1379, the necessity to replace a deceased Abbot arose again, and this time the Prior and convent of the Abbey received the King's permission to elect their sub-Prior, John of Timworth. This was clearly not a unanimous decision, for the Abbey records show the orders for the arrest of another monk, named Edmund Bromefield. It seems that Brother Edmund had schemed with fifteen other monks to have Brother John's appointment annulled, despite the fact that it had received royal assent.

Brother Edmund, with another Brother, John of Medenham, and fourteen others, plus various clerks and laymen had conspired to wrestle control of the Abbey from the elected Abbot. Somehow Edmund had managed to get himself made the Pope's nominee. The Earls of March and Suffolk and the Sheriff of Suffolk had to be sent in to arrest Brother Edmund and his co-conspirators for this blatant contempt of the Crown. However, it took another five years before the Pope gave way and allowed John of Timworth to take up the Abbacy.

Clearly, peace did not always reign within the Abbey's walls.

The daily routines of the Abbey – work, worship, prayer and the production of gorgeous illustrated manuscripts

– were punctuated by the regular excitements of the elections of Abbots and the royal visits of Kings and their retinues. In 1383, Richard II paid a ten-day visit to the Abbey with Anne of Bohemia and put the Abbey to huge expense. Later, it was the turn of Henry VI, who extended his stay from Christmas of 1443 to St George's Day of the following year.

Henry's visit was a magnificent affair. The Abbot employed an extra eighty masons and others to set about enlarging and improving the Abbey's lodgings for the occasion. In the event, a huge crowd of 500 townsmen, headed by the aldermen and the burgesses, joined the Abbot and the monks in a mass turnout to greet the young King. The whole town must have been there. Even the Bishop of

Parliament in the Abbey at Bury.

Norwich ceased hostilities and came to join with the Abbot in giving his royal highness a double blessing. The King dismounted from his horse and the two ecclesiastics united in anointing him with holy water.

In 1446, the King's Parliament assembled in Bury, transferring their business temporarily from London to the great refectory hall of the Abbey. Humphrey, the Duke of Gloucester, had been ordered to attend and on his arrival he was arrested on a charge of high treason. He was kept under guard in his lodgings at St Saviour's hospital, one of five Abbey hospitals established in Bury. However, before the Duke could face his trial he was found dead in his bed.

There were no marks of violence on his body and his death was attributed to an attack of apoplexy or a heart attack. This seemed very convenient for a man with powerful friends, whose trial might have seen him cleared of all charges. The fact that the trial had already been moved out of London had given rise to comment, and now popular opinion decided that Duke Humphrey had been murdered.

It was an event which eventually gave rise to the story of the ghostly Grey Lady. Ghostly monks and spectral nuns are virtually inseparable from the sites of crumbling churches, graveyards and ancient monastic ruins. When the night is black as pitch and the wintry wind shivers and groans, fevered imaginations will grasp at every movement and shadow. The tormented souls of the long dead, we instinctively feel, could rise to walk or glide between and

St Saviour's Hospital, where Humphrey the Duke of Gloucester was found dead.

through the haunted pillars and frost-glittering stones. The remains of the old Abbey at Bury St Edmunds are no exception to this rule, and here there are many spooky tales to be told.

The Brown Monk and the Grey Lady are both said to haunt the Abbey ruins and the town, although it may be that there are many brown monks and many grey nuns who have all merged

45

their disembodied wanderings into the basic legend: one ghost monk could look very like another in his coarse cowl and robe, and who could hope to tell nuns apart when they choose to glide swiftly and silently through solid walls with their faces shadowed?

Duke Humphrey may have had a heart attack, but all the talk was of poison and a royal assassination. Who could have administered the poison? Suspicion fell upon a young nun named Maude Carew. The story goes that Maude had taken her vows and entered Fornham Prior to pursue her lover, who had become a monk at the Abbey. The man she loved had not returned her passion and had instead become Father Bernard, a devout monastic scholar. Maude had determined that she could not let him go, and to follow him into Holy Orders was the only way to continue.

Duke Humphrey's trial was to be held in Bury St Edmunds and Father Bernard was to be called as a prosecution witness. The naïve Maude was apparently deceived into believing that this would place her beloved in grave danger. Any man who spoke against the Duke, she was told, could be sure of a swift and terrible revenge if and when he was acquitted.

This was the story that prompted the obsessed Maude to do the royal dirty work. Henry's Queen, Margaret of Anjou, is said to be the one who summoned the nun. Maude then used an underground tunnel which was said to link either the Abbey or the Priory to the hospital and so gained entry to Duke Humphrey's room. She dripped deadly poison into his lips and fled.

One version of the story then has her losing herself in the underground labyrinth. Somehow, either by accident or remorse, she managed to swallow what was left of the poison, and finally emerged to fall, dying, into the arms of Father Bernard. The good father then cursed her for her evil act and condemned her to wander between the worlds of the living and the dead for ever more.

According to the legend, Maude Carew is now the Grey Lady, the spectral nun who haunts the Abbey precincts and the town, and Father Bernard is possibly the Brown Monk. Perhaps he came to regret his curse? Perhaps now they are now looking for forgiveness, or for each other.

Either way, their shades have been reported many times and in many places. The Abbey ruins and the great churchyard seem to be their favourite haunts, especially on 24 February, the anniversary of Duke Humphrey's dubious demise.

At other times their shades have been glimpsed or heard in such diverse locations as the Nutshell pub, the Grapes, Cupola House, the Angel and the Old Suffolk Hotel. Bridewell Lane, Athenaeum Lane, and Fornham Road also have their own collection of unexplained knocking sounds, footsteps, movements or just sudden icy chills.

In addition to the Brown Monk and the Grey Lady, King Edmund himself is said to haunt the old Abbey. The ghost of the last Abbot is said to haunt the Dog and Partridge, his last lodging after he was turned out of the Abbey at the

The ruins of St Edmund's Abbey.

Dissolution. Once he is said to have manifested briefly wearing his mitre before he simply faded away.

The Fordham Priory is now the Priory Hotel and a fragment of the old St Saviour's hospital still stands on Fordham Road behind Tesco, but there has never been any sign of any tunnel between them, or of a tunnel to the Abbey.

Anyway, these royal visits – and the gossip and intrigues which accompanied them – were the highlights of life at the great monastery, and in between the never-ending flow of ordinary pilgrims continued to arrive to pay their respects to the shrine of the saint. The miracles seem to have petered out. The last one recorded was when a man named Symon Brown was miraculously saved from drowning at sea. He was rescued after shouting desperate prayers and vows in Edmund's name. The miracles and the curse of St Edmund may have faded into history, but the pulling power of his holy shrine remained.

ABOVE *The ruins of St Saviour's hospital are a prime site for haunting.*

TOP *The Athenaeum.*

THE GUILDHALL

The Bury St Edmunds Guildhall dates back to the thirteenth century, although it was largely rebuilt in the fifteenth century. It was built by the townspeople for the aldermen and mayor who formed the town council, and has always played an important role in the town's history. While the Abbey kept its firm monastic hold over the town's business, the Guildhall was always the focus of opposition. From here, the long struggle was waged for the town's independence, and during the violent dispute of 1327 the Prior and several monks were kept locked up in the Guildhall for several days.

The Bury Guildhall.

The Nutshell, the smallest pub in England – and it's haunted.

As the winds whipped through the interior of the great monastery, every lamp and candle was snuffed out, plunging the monks into confusion and darkness. Only one light, which was kept burning constantly before the Blessed Sacrement, was spared. From this all of the others were subsequently re-kindled, but we can imagine the pandemonium among the monks before the candles were restored and the darkness diminished.

In the same year, more storms brought rising floods: the River Lark burst its banks and spilt its swollen rainwater into the Abbey precincts. The flood waters rose high enough to float a boat in the naves of the great church and St James' church and in the lay chapel of the crypt.

However, the worst was yet to come. On the 24 January 1465, another disaster was to overtake the luckless monks and their re-built Abbey. A major fire started in the western bell tower and swiftly swept through the transepts. The monks watched in horror as flames engulfed the spire of the tower. At first they feared that the spire was going to topple and crash down across the transepts and the nave, the very heart of the church, but then, like a closing telescope, they saw the spire sink down into the tower itself.

The tower must have been at least the height of the modern cathedral and an imaginative drawing by W.K. Hardy suggests it may have been even higher. It would have been a staggering achievement for medieval times, visible for many miles out into the flat surrounding countryside to inspire the pilgrims as they made their approach.

The saint's powers of protection must also have been on the wane, for the Abbey was not exempt from the power of the elements and the ravages of flood and storm. In January of 1439, a violent tempest smashed its way across Suffolk and severely damaged the town and the Abbey when it struck Bury St Edmunds. The bell tower of the Abbey was rocked, and the glazing of all the windows was shattered.

Fire-fighting in the Middle Ages was a hopeless affair. There would have been nothing that the monks could do except to try and carry some of their treasures clear of the inferno, or perhaps form a leather bucket chain from the River Lark. Desperate monks would have stood in sodden robes, passing filled buckets from the river along a sweating human chain, to be hurled onto the roaring flames. Other monks would have been dashing to and fro, trying to rescue what could be saved. Some would have simply wept and prayed.

At one stage it was said that King Edmund's shrine was walled with flames like a furnace. If the saint's sacred body was still intact and uncorrupted by this stage then almost certainly it was cremated: only the bones would have been recoverable. The great Abbey of Bury St Edmunds was no stranger to pillage and ruin, but this time the disaster must have seemed total and final.

AD 1539

THE RUIN
OF THE ABBEY

OR MORE THAN five centuries, the great Abbey of St Edmund dominated the town that also bore his name. It was part of an enduring triumvirate of power: the King in his palace, the baron in his castle and the Church holding an iron-clad, spiritual grip on them all. Politics was a three-way wrestling match. The economy, before the rise of the merchants, was wholly dependent on the way the Abbots and the barons managed their vast holdings of land.

Cracks were beginning to show in this entrenched feudal world, but the basic structure and the underlying pattern of life and power remained the same. And then the unthinkable happened: almost overnight, one of the central players was removed. By royal decree, the great religious institutions were brought crashing down, and the magnificent Abbeys and Priories which once thrust their proud towers as high as any castle keep were reduced to decay and ruin. King Henry VIII had ordered the Dissolution of the Monasteries.

The shock, especially among the communities of monks, must have been profound. The old way of life had gone forever, and could never return.

In order to divorce his wife, Henry broke with Rome – and the ripples were enormous. He called a special parliament to rush through a series of laws to sever all links, and to stop payment of all the special taxes that had been due to the Pope. For good measure he added a Treason Act, which threatened anyone who tried to deny his authority over the reformed Church with death.

These measures had quite a lot of popular support. The poor had grown resentful of the Church and its enormous wealth. In 1536, Henry ordered his vicar general, Thomas Cromwell, to assess the actual wealth of all the religious houses. That same year he ordered many 'dissolved': their wealth – and all the value of their holdings and lands – went to the Crown.

ABOVE *Remains of the old monastery at Bury, showing what a magnificent sight it must once have been. ('In 1773,' the caption to this Regency picture adds, 'the embalmed body of Thomas Beaufort, son of John of Gaunt, was discovered here by some labourers, as perfect as the day of his dissolution.')*

LEFT *The ruins today.*

53

THE LIBRARY MANUSCRIPTS

The Abbey library is said to have been one of the most magnificent in Europe, with over 2,000 illustrated manuscripts. The monks of Bury St Edmunds were famous for their meticulous and brilliant artwork. Most of the books would have been written and painted on vellum, the most expensive form of calf-skin parchment. Gorgeous flowing capitals would have headed every chapter with decorative marginal pictures. Where these have survived, the pigments used by the medieval monks are as bright and glowing today as when they were originally painted. Many of these priceless books simply vanished. Some of them may have been hidden or disposed of when the monks realised that the evil day was almost upon them. Others may have been simply overlooked because the King's looters were not interested in anything that could not be quickly converted into hard cash. Many of the Bibles would have been decorated with gold or silver, but if there were no precious jewels or metals attached to the binding then their value may not have been recognised. An alderman of Ipswich is said to have acquired 100 or more of the manuscripts sometime during the next century. A few others are now in museums. The Bury Bible is at Corpus Christi in Cambridge. A few other Bury manuscripts are in the British Museum, and a beautiful *Picture Book of the Life and Miracles of St Edmund* is in the Metropolitan Museum of New York.

The British Museum, where some of the Abbey's manuscripts may now be found. (Library of Congress, Prints & Photographs Division, LC-DIG-ppmsc-08563)

The treasure flowed into the royal coffers, and Henry couldn't get his greedy hands on enough. In 1539, he went all the way and ordered the Dissolution of all the larger monasteries, including the great Abbey of Bury St Edmunds.

The last Abbot of Bury St Edmunds was John Reeve of Melford, sometimes known as John Melford. He was elected in 1513, the thirty-second Abbot. In November of 1535, four of Thomas Cromwell's deputies appeared at John's Abbey to make their first inventory of its lands and treasures. They were also looking for stories of crimes or broken vows to discredit the monks with and to provide further excuses for what was to come; however, it seems that on this occasion they were disappointed. They could not find much to discredit the reigning Abbot or his monks, save that they enjoyed dice and cards and did not preach much.

The Abbot managed to hold off Cromwell's men for a short while by renewing Cromwell's lease on a farm property owned by the Abbey, and including a bribe of £10 a year for Cromwell and his son. However, it was not enough to keep the wolves at bay for long: the smaller religious houses were already being vandalised, and soon it would be the turn of the great monasteries.

In 1538 the assault on the Abbey of St Edmund began. The Keeper of the King's Jewels, Sir John Williams, and three others arrived to start the systematic looting of the Abbey's treasures.

The found a rich shrine which they described as 'very difficult to deface', but they hauled away a magnificent hoard of gold and silver, an emerald embossed cross and many other jewels of great value.

There is no record of what sort of resistance the monks made, but no doubt the royal looters took with them a strong force of men-at-arms to see the job through.

In November of the following year, the Abbot, the Prior and forty of the monks were forced to sign a 'deed of surrender', which effectively meant that they could now be thrown out of the Abbey. The buildings themselves were then brutally plundered and cannibalised. The valuable lead was stripped from the roof and carried away, along with the great bells that had once tolled for the many prayers. The church and its buildings were now fully exposed to the elements, and rain and storms eventually rotted the bare roof timbers, causing them to collapse. Slowly the pillars and walls fell into ruin, and the crypt and the nave of the great Abbey church were buried in rubble. Eventually even the rubble itself was sold by the cartload, and the eager townspeople carried it away to build more of their own homes.

The great gates and the two smaller churches of St Mary's and St James' somehow survived to be used as parish churches. Of all the rest, only parts of the Abbot's palace and the old Abbot's bridge remained intact.

The displaced monks were given secular livings or small pensions, but the last Abbot did not live long enough to draw a single payment.

Three views of the town.

THE CHARNEL HOUSE

The ruins of the Charnel House stand in the centre of the great churchyard, surrounded by neat black iron railings. It was built in the twelfth century to store the old bones that had been dug up from the graveyard in order to make room for fresh burials.

There are some interesting memorial plaques which can still be read. One is to Bartholomew Gosnold, the Suffolk explorer and sea captain who carried the first English settlers to North America. Another is the only memorial to Sarah Lloyd, who was hanged in Bury St Edmunds at the turn of the nineteenth century, when the crime of theft was one of 200 hanging offences. Sarah was a young maid who made the mistake of letting her boyfriend into the house where she was working. Together they stole some trinkets and tried to set fire to the house. The boyfriend was acquitted at their trial, but poor Sarah was found guilty and hanged.

Many of the senior monks were not interred in the Charnel House but buried underneath the Abbey. In 1930, the graves of five Abbots were excavated from the floor of the chapter house and their skeletons uncovered. In one of the stone coffins were the remains of Abbot Samson.

The charnel house in the great churchyard.

The Dog and Partridge, where the last Abbot lived his last days.

Abbot John moved into lodgings in what is now the Dog and Partridge pub in Westgate Street, only a stone's throw away from the Abbey. From there he could witness the total desecration of his once proud monastery, and within a few months he was dead – of a broken heart, according to some.

Abbot John was buried in the chancel of St Mary's church, with a simple brass nameplate and a Latin epitaph over his remains. Later the brass plate was stolen and his grave slab was broken up to make room for another burial.

One major mystery remains. When the King's officers first arrived to investigate the Abbey treasures, they found that the venerated bones of the saint had already vanished from the shrine behind the great altar.

One theory is that perhaps there were no bones. All that remained of St Edmund could have been consumed in the Great Fire, and perhaps the senior monks then played a medieval con trick and simply pretended that there was still a body, or at least a skeleton, inside the rebuilt shrine.

If that was the case, there would have been no need to continue to keep the secret after the shrine had been demolished. The more popular theory is that the monks must have had plenty of warning of what was coming, and had used it to open up the coffin and hide whatever it contained.

Nobody knows where the monks concealed their sacred relics. They have never been found. However, it is tempting to wonder what options might have gone through the minds of Abbot John and his senior advisers when they knew that the King's men were on the way to loot their precious trust. Where could they hide St Edmund's bones?

One possible answer springs to mind. The Abbey had its own adjacent churchyard, and where better to hide one set of bones than in a graveyard that was already filled with hundreds of skeletons? Perhaps the great churchyard has a secret to keep, and St Edmund's bones may not have moved very far.

BURNING THE PROTESTANT MARTYRS

WHEN HENRY VIII died in 1547 he had at last achieved his goal: he left three children, and one of them was a son. Nine-year-old Edward became Edward VI under the protectorate of the Duke of Somerset. This meant, in effect, that England was still ruled by the same circle of old men who had supported Henry, and so the Reformation continued. The plundering of the monasteries' assets for the Crown went on as before. The new Protestant religion was enforced, and the first English prayer book became the official text for all religious services. Unfortunately, however, Edward was a sickly King, and he died six years later of tuberculosis.

Before he died, Edward named Lady Jane Grey, Henry VIII's granddaughter, as his successor. His sister, Mary, disagreed: she gathered an army at Framlingham Castle and – with most of the Suffolk and Norfolk gentry behind her – she marched on London, displaced Lady Jane and had her condemned to death. In true British tradition of the times, Lady Jane's head was eventually chopped off.

Mary Tudor was now Queen of England – and she was a very bitter woman, with a lot of axes to grind. She was determined to reunite the English Church with Rome. She began by cancelling all the religious laws of her father and her brother's reign; then she married her cousin, Phillip, who was the heir to the throne of Spain. Phillip became the joint ruler

Jane Grey's signature scratched into the prison wall.

THE ELIZABETHAN MARTYRS

Bloody Mary died in 1558, and her sister Elizabeth inherited the throne of England. Elizabeth was a staunch Protestant, and the priests had to go back to using the English prayer book.

Many priests at the time were turning with the tide, hiding their Catholic sacraments and vestments when they were supposed to be Protestant and hiding the English prayer book when they were supposed to be Catholic.

However, these were confused times and in Bury there were to be two more Protestant martyrs. Those who were executed during the reign of Queen Mary were generally known as the Marian martyrs. Those executed during the reign of Elizabeth became the Elizabethan martyrs.

Many ministers refused to conform to the official Protestant Church of England teachings. One of those, who continued to loudly voice his own opinions, was the Revd John Copping. He was jailed on remand for seven years and eventually he was joined by another minister named Elias Thacker. Together their preaching was seen to be undermining the good order in the jail, so they were sent to trial in 1583 for distributing Puritan literature and supporting independency. They were also accused of some serious seditious graffiti which had appeared in St Mary's church. They were found guilty and received the death penalty.

Today in Bury St Edmunds, in a small courtyard in front of the United Reformed Church in Whiting street, there stands another small, weathered grey stone obelisk. The inscription on this monument reads:

> In memory of Elias Thacker and John Copping, who were hanged in this town on the 4th and 5th of June 1585 respectively, for disseminating the principles of independence.

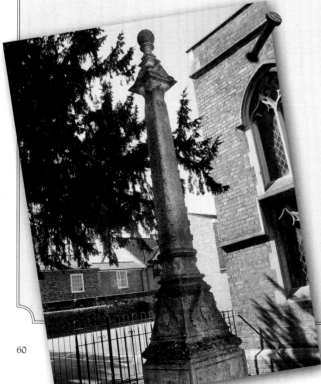

The memorial to the Elizabethan Martyrs.

of England, and the country was now in alliance with one of the major Catholic powers of Europe. Inevitably there was Protestant opposition. (The very word 'Protestant' describes those Christians who protested against Papal jurisdiction.)

During Mary's reign, at least 280 Protestant martyrs were burned to death. Those who were found guilty of heresy were tied to stakes and surrounded by piles of brushwood, which were then set on fire. This was a slow and agonising way to die. First the heat and smoke would rise to choke their lungs and scorch their flesh; then the flames would roar up high and burn them alive. These fiery spectacles drew huge crowds.

All of this brings us back to Bury St Edmunds, where at least nineteen Protestant martyrs were burned at the stake.

One of the first churchmen to be burned, and the first to be burned in Suffolk, was Rowland Taylor. He was the rector of Hadleigh, a town about 30 miles from Bury, but one of the many church appointments he held was that of Archdeacon of Bury St Edmunds, where he had preached sermons in favour of the new ways of worship.

Taylor had also incurred Mary's wrath by supporting Lady Jane Grey during her fleeting accession to the throne. He had also taken advantage of the new shift in the rules of faith to get married and enjoy a family life with his wife and children. Mary's swing back to the old rules of the Catholic Church meant that he had to give up either his wife or his living. Clerical celibacy was one of the injustices against which he preached at Bury.

Taylor was arrested and imprisoned while a commission of bishops and lawyers instituted the legal proceedings against him. He refused to recant, giving instead a fervent defence of clerical marriage. Finally he was excommunicated and sentenced to death. The sentence was carried out at his own rectory at Hadleigh, on Aldham Common, just outside the town.

He died bravely, and although stripped of his clerical garments he gave one last sermon from the stake. His wife, two daughters and a son were there to receive his blessing and watch him die; their anguish can hardly be imagined.

'Bloody' Mary Tudor.

61

GUNPOWDER AND TREASON

Another Suffolk man who could be said to have been hanged for his beliefs was Ambrose Rookfield, from the village of Stanningfield in the modern-day Borough of Bury St Edmunds. Rookfield was a staunch Catholic and one of the small group of conspirators who plotted to blow up the Houses of Parliament in London.

The Gunpowder Plot aimed to fill one of the cellars below the Houses of Parliament with barrels of gunpowder so they could blow up the building and all those within it, killing the Protestant King. Guy Fawkes has become generally known for this, but he was only the mercenary hired to place the powder barrels. Rookwood was one of the chief financiers, and not only supplied much of the money for powder and weapons but also the transport and communications, by way of his excellent stable of horses.

The plot failed when one of the conspirators sent a warning note to one of the Catholic ministers due to attend the planned opening ceremony of Parliament. The letter was passed to the King, the cellars were searched and Guy Fawkes discovered with the powder barrels.

The rest of the plotters fled. Rookwood was the last to leave London, but he escaped using a relay of his best horses. The conspirators were all eventually captured, and Rookwood was hanged at Westminster Yard alongside Fawkes and two other members of the gang.

At the scaffold, the Suffolk man made a speech which brought many in the crowd to tears. He confessed to his crime but prayed for God to bless the King and turn him into a good Catholic.

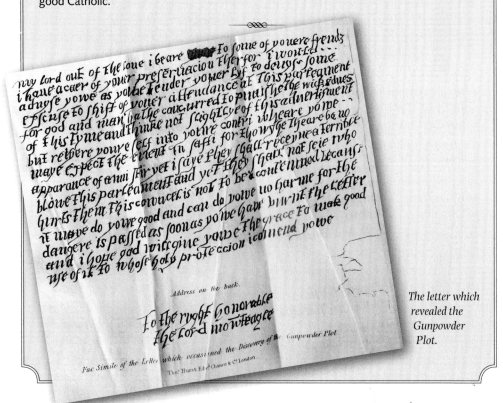

The letter which revealed the Gunpowder Plot.

The Gunpowder conspirators immediately after they were captured.

The vault beneath Parliament where the gunpowder was placed.

The memorial to the Protestant martyrs.

Murder Most Foul

THINGOE HILL TODAY is a small industrial site tucked close beside the bridge carrying the A14 over Fornham Road in Bury St Edmunds. However, in the past it played a much more important role. In the Middle Ages it was a Moot Hill, a meeting place for the Court for the Hundred of Thingoe, one of the Suffolk Hundreds which comprised eighteen parishes, including Bury. In the eighteenth century the court was moved to a site in Great Barton, and Thingoe Hill, then a grassy mound on the edge of town, became Bury's place of execution.

The hangings carried out here could draw vast crowds. Condemned criminals, burglars, horse thieves, sheep stealers, murderers and highwaymen were all hanged on this spot. The witches denounced by Mathew Hopkins in 1644 were hanged here, following two more accused old women from Lowestoft who had been tried and found guilty of witchcraft in 1642. Perhaps they were the lucky ones, in that they had not been condemned to be burned at the stake. These were cruel and superstitious times.

One notorious trial and hanging which caught the public interest was that of a man named Arundel Coke in 1722. Coke was a barrister and one of the pillars of local society. Unfortunately, like many others he invested heavily in the so-called South Sea Bubble and found himself facing financial ruin when the scam was revealed.

He could only see one solution to his problem. His brother-in-law Edward Crisp was a wealthy man, and Coke believed that if Crisp were to die then his fortune would be inherited by his sister. Through his wife, Coke would get his hands on Crisp's money.

Coke plotted with a local handyman named Edmund Woodburn who was prepared to do the job. Coke had a house on Honey Hill and, after a New Year's Eve party there, he led Crisp through the great churchyard on the pretence of visiting a coffee shop in the town. On the way, as pre-arranged, Woodburn leapt out of the

The great churchyard where Edward Crisp was attacked.

darkness and attacked Crisp with a knife. Coke fled, and left Crisp to his fate.

Woodburn proved a clumsy would-be murderer. Crisp survived with a cut nose and both Woodburn and Coke were arrested and brought to trial. Found guilty, they were both hanged on Thingoe Hill.

Another hanging which drew huge crowds was that of John and Nathan Nichols, a father and son who had murdered Sarah Nichols. The true horror of this family crime was that John was the father of Sarah and Nathan was her brother. The judge called it a monstrous depravity for a father to instigate one of his children to murder another.

The girl was seventeen years old and her body was discovered in a ditch close to the Fox Inn at Honington. She had been beaten over the head with a fence stake and then strangled with one of her own garters. The family had lived in the parish of Fakenham and it soon became apparent to the local community that this was a crime within the family circle. Even the girl's step-mother seemed to be making only pretence of any sort of grief.

The father and son were both arrested, whereupon Nathan confessed to having killed his sister under orders from his father. The younger man claimed as his defence that he was too frightened of his father to disobey.

John Nichols was a man of sixty and a carpenter on the estate of the Duke of Grafton. His son Nathan was under twenty and John's second wife was apparently not much older than the unfortunate Sarah. One can only guess at the sexual tensions and jealousies which must have contaminated the household and provoked the scenario for murder.

Father and son were both found guilty of their crime and hanged together at Honington, where the murder took place, on 26 March 1794. Afterwards John Nichols was left to hang in chains upon the spot, while Nathan was taken down to be dissected. The gibbet cage used to hang John Nichols was dug up on Honington airfield many years later and can now be seen as an exhibit in Moyse's Hall Museum.

The last person to be hanged at Thingoe hill was a woman named Elizabeth Burroughs, who was convicted of the wilful murder of Mary Booty on 18 March 1776.

Hangings still continued outside the old gaol on the Sudbury Road and on the

Market Hill, and there is one particularly gruesome murder associated with Bury St Edmunds which has become a classic of true-crime history. The murderer was hanged outside the new gaol and drew one of the biggest crowds ever recorded. The case is the notorious murder of Maria Marten in the Red Barn.

The perpetrator of the foul deed was a man named William Corder, who came from a wealthy farming family. The grim and tragic story occurred in the small scattered village of Polstead near Stoke-by-Nayland, but Corder was subsequently tried and hanged at Bury St Edmunds. His death mask is still preserved in the Moyse's Hall Museum which overlooks the ancient Buttermarket.

Maria was a mole-catcher's daughter, which was a social level or two below her lover; Corder therefore tried to conduct their romantic affair in secret. Unfortunately, Maria fell pregnant and bore him a son. The child died soon after birth, but no doubt it set the village tongues a'wagging.

Maria was aiming for a wedding and the elevated status of marriage, but obviously that was not on her lover's agenda. However, Corder did make known his offer to elope to Ipswich with her to be married by licence. Maria left her home to meet Corder at the Red Barn. Later Corder told her family that she had travelled to Ipswich and was waiting for him to join her there.

WILLIAM CORDER.

MARIA MARTEN.

THOMAS HENRY,
Maria Marten's Child.

Portraits of William Corder,
Maria Marten and Thomas Henry.

Maria Marten's Cottage.

Soon Corder left the district, telling everyone that he was going to join Maria in Ipswich and from there sending regular letters to maintain the fiction that she was still alive.

He had, of course, murdered the unfortunate Maria and buried her body in the Red Barn. He might even have got away with it, but then came the paranormal twist that has kept the story alive and fascinating through all the following years. Maria's mother began to be haunted by a vivid and re-occurring dream in which she actually saw her daughter being killed and then interred in a hastily dug grave inside the Red Barn.

It was a bizarre, horrific and unbelievable tale, and no doubt her husband initially considered it to be no more than a nightmare. Eventually, however, the distraught woman persuaded him to go to the barn and dig up the earth floor.

Perhaps the first few spades of earth were loose enough to cause him some misgiving. He dug on, and suddenly the spade pulled up the corner of a shawl which he recognized with horror as Maria's. He continued until he struck the body, and then he fled from the barn.

The mortified parent could not continue the task but he raised the alarm and other men completed the excavation of the body. The remains were confirmed as those of his daughter.

By this time Corder had wisely left Ipswich, but he was eventually tracked down to the London borough of Ealing. There he had married, assumed an air of respectability, and was running a school for young ladies. No doubt he loudly protested his innocence, but he was arrested and brought back to Bury St Edmunds to be flung into the town gaol to await his punishment.

The medical evidence at the trial showed that Maria had been murdered by a combination of shooting and stabbing; she had then been buried while still alive. Such a brutal and frenzied attack on a helpless young girl roused a huge amount of moral anger and morbid fascination and there were riots when the trial was held. Thousands of people wanted to attend, and the unruly mob held up the swearing of the jury and the proceedings in general.

Finally the trial got under way. Corder claimed that Maria had committed suicide, although how he hoped to explain the fact that she had stabbed and shot herself is not clear. He did admit to burying the body in an act of panic when he realized that he would be blamed for her death. The jury were not impressed, however, and found him guilty. The judge sentenced him to death.

An estimated crowd of 70,000 turned out to see the hanging. About 70 percent of the population of Bury were there, and people had trekked in for miles from the surrounding countryside.

Corder was left swinging on the spot for an hour, which was customary to give everyone a chance to gawp at the spectacle. Then the body was taken down and again placed on public view at the Shire Hall. Finally it was given up for medical dissection, which was quite often the last gruesome penalty to be extracted from executed criminals.

The dubious distinction of being the last person to be publicly hanged in Bury actually went to a young lady named Catherine Foster, after what came to be known as the case of the poisoned dumplings. She was hanged on the 17 April 1847. An estimated crowd of 10,000 flocked to see her swing, but although

The execution of William Corder outside Bury Gaol on 11 August 1828.

The Town Gaol

Throughout the eighteenth century, convicted criminals and those awaiting trial were locked up in the old Moyse's Hall. Those who could afford a shilling a week could pay for a bed and a sheet on the ground floor; those who could not were confined in barrack besteads down in the dungeon. Debtors had better treatment and bedrooms on the upper floor.

It was all inadequate by 1805, and so the new County Gaol was built in Sicklesmere Road. This was progress, and the new jail became a model institution for the whole county. Prison uniforms and chains were abolished in 1818 and prisoners were even encouraged to learn to read and write.

The Bury gaol was finally closed in 1880 and most of it was demolished, except for the governor's house and the massive, high-walled gateway.

Catherine Foster was the last woman to be hanged in public; the last man hanged inside the gaol was George Carnt in 1851. Carnt's crime was the wilful murder of Elizabeth Bainbridge of the village of Lawshall.

Carnt was a twenty-three-year-old farm labourer, given to epileptic fits and heavy drinking. Elizabeth was a young married woman of twenty-nine who had been abandoned by her husband. In the quaint court language of the time, it was known that the accused had been 'desirous of forming intimacy with the deceased'.

The two had been drinking brandy and water together in the Harrow Inn at Lawshall at midday. They left the public house together and were last seen walking across a field together. It was the last time Elizabeth was seen alive.

Later in the evening Carnt returned to the Harrow alone. He was dirty and wet and had lost his hat. When asked where his hat had gone, he replied, 'In the pond.' He was also asked, 'Where was Elizabeth?' and had no answer. A quick check showed that Elizabeth had not returned to her home. A search began by lantern light and Elizabeth's dead body was eventually fished out of the pond by a policeman.

There was a large bruise on the dead woman's face which was taken as evidence of a quarrel and a blow. Carnt may not have intended to kill Elizabeth, but he was tried, found guilty and hanged for her murder.

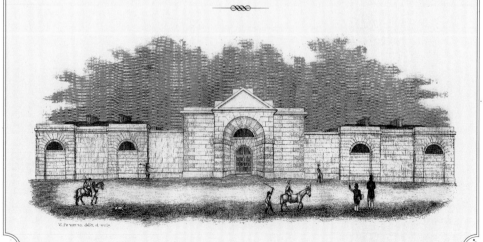

W. Benson, delt. et sculp.

many of them still enjoyed the public spectacle, others were beginning to feel that for a modern nineteenth-century society these events were a disgusting reminder of a medieval past best conducted in private.

Catherine's crime was a fairly common one. She was a woman who had married too young and too soon. Marriage in haste and repentance at leisure was not for her. Within a matter of weeks she had decided that her new husband had to go. She chose the easiest method to hand: she poisoned his food. In this case, it was arsenic in his dumplings.

John Foster was a fit and sturdy young farm labourer. He came home to his good wife after a hard day's work with a hearty appetite. He was ready for his evening meal, and if he noticed anything wrong with the taste he was probably too hungry to care. He ate most of it before the arsenic had its first effect and he was violently sick.

John rushed out into the cottage yard to throw up as much as he could of his dinner. For the rest of the night John was violently ill with vomiting and diarrhoea – and he was dead within twenty-four hours.

Catherine carefully collected up the vomited food and threw it with the rest of the uneaten meal into the next meadow. Unfortunately, however, the poisoned remains were quickly found by some chickens which happily pecked them up, and by a cat which was also too hungry to miss out on a free meal. The next day the chickens and the cat all lay dead on

OPPOSITE *Front view of Bury Gaol.*

BELOW *The town gaol on Sicklesmere Road today.*

The Highwaymen

The first Royal Mail stagecoach services to and from Bury St Edmunds started in 1737. The Angel Hotel and the Greyhound in the Buttermarket were the two main coaching inns with extensive stables. The 'Old Bury' ran three times a week from the Angel to London. The coach from the Greyhound took two days and went through Braintree. The Three Tuns in Crown Street was the coaching inn for the Norwich Mercury. The major roads became Turnpike Roads and tolls were charged.

The eighteenth century was a century of hard winters and so our popular Christmas card pictures of Dickensian coaches rattling through flying snowstorms and frozen village landscapes were probably not far from the reality of the time. Charles Dickens and the portly Pickwick both stayed at the Angel, where there was always a welcoming cup of mulled ale or wine to thaw out red faces and chilled bones.

Dick Turpin is the epitome of the highwayman and he is said to have visited the lovely old black-timbered and cream-painted Bell Inn at Kentford, halfway between Bury and Newmarket. A coaching inn was always a good haunt for highwaymen, the ideal place to surreptitiously assess the plunder value of any particular group of passengers. Nearby Newmarket Heath was also a prime hunting ground for highway robbers: there they could find rich gentlemen on their way to lose money at the races or lucky winners carrying their spoils home. In 1795 the problem reached the point where some people were calling for armed guards to be put on the mail coaches, although this never happened.

The popular image of the highwayman is that of a romantic horseman, usually pictured in a black cocked hat, cape and mask with a brace of pistols in his hands. Fiction would have him the bored son of a nobleman only there for the thrill and the sport, or a shadowy vicar relieving the rich of their ill-gotten gains to fill the church collecting plate. 'Stand and deliver, your money or your life,' they are supposed to have said.

In truth, the highwayman was more likely a black-hearted ruffian or some poverty-stricken wretch who saw no choice but a life of crime. His actual words would have been more like, 'Give us yer bleedin' money or I'll blow yer bleedin' head orf.'

Many of the unsuccessful ones did their last dance on the end of the gallows rope at Bury St Edmunds, either at Thingoe Hill or the old gaol.

---

the field. To coin a pun, it was a dead give-away.

Post mortems were conducted on the husband and one of the chickens and traces of arsenic were found in both stomachs. More traces of the poison were found on the cloth that had wrapped up John's dumpling. The case was conclusive. Catherine was tried for the wilful murder of her husband, found guilty and hanged on the Market Hill in Bury St Edmunds.

Today the town boundaries of Bury St Edmunds have expanded beyond Thingoe Hill. All you will find there are business premises, a builder's yard – and, ironically, a health and fitness club and gymnasium. The hangings, the cheering crowds and the condemned man in the gibbet cage are all images lost in the past.

The burning of Cranmer, perhaps Mary's most famous victim.

A local butcher was ordered to light the faggots piled around the condemned man, but he refused. A lighted brand was thrown and the fire was eventually lit. However, one of the duty guards took sympathy on the condemned man and struck him across the head with his halberd, a long staff topped with a steel spike and an axe blade. The blow killed Taylor and spared him the worst of his agony.

Taylor was the third Protestant martyr to be burned, and the first in Suffolk. However, hundreds more were to follow. The first executions were all of senior churchmen, but then the whole business got out of hand. Those burned in Bury St Edmunds included a sawyer, a labourer, a wheelwright, a husbandman, two weavers and a servant of the Crown. The range of victims was wide and filtered down through all classes. They were all executed on Thingoe Hill, a small hill just outside the town which was the normal gathering place for the spectacle of burnings and hangings.

Today there is a small white monument on Aldham Common which marks the spot where Rowland Taylor was burned to death. It is fenced in by neat, black iron railings. In a peaceful corner of the old churchyard, facing the green and the cathedral in the Abbey gardens at Bury St Edmunds, there is another memorial to the Protestant martyrs who were burned in the town.

At the base of the small obelisk are the words:

In Loving memory of the seventeen Protestant martyrs who for their faithful testimony to God's truth during the reign of Queen Mary suffered death in this town 1555-1558.

Carved below are the words:

The Noble Army of Martyrs Praise Thee, O God.

The names of the victims are listed on the two sides of the base, and upon the back of the monument the simple inscription:

They loved not their lives unto death.

Their courage and commitment to their faith is commemorated, but nowhere is there any memorial to Queen Mary Tudor, who became generally known as Bloody Mary, or the most evil woman in history.

AD 1662

WITCH MANIA

IN LOWESTOFT, IN the year 1662, a strange and horrible event was witnessed: a toad fell out of a child's coarse woollen blanket, causing his mother to scream. She called for her eldest son to throw the loathsome creature on to the fire, and the boy obeyed. The bloated and wart-riddled body hit the flames, screeching and sizzling, and then vanished with a hissing pop like a small explosion. Later, old Amy Denny, who was thought to be a witch, was discovered cowering and cursing in her cottage; scorch marks and burns were found all over her body.

This was the horrifying tale told to the Court of County Assizes in Bury St Edmunds. There were two elderly widows on trial for their lives, accused of witchcraft. One was Amy Denny, and the other was Rose Cullender.

The case was heard in Bury St Edmunds because, at that time, Bury was the largest town in Suffolk, and the seat of the county court. The women had tried to buy herrings from

a Lowestoft fish merchant named Samuel Pacey, and had gone off muttering and complaining when they were refused. Soon afterwards, Pacey's two daughters began to suffer from fits and violent stomach pains, and it was readily believed that the family had been cursed.

All the children involved were pitifully ill at the trial and seemed to be struck dumb, but their parents spoke up for them. The Pacey girls, plus a third child, had repeatedly vomited up pins and nails. This, it was alleged, the witches had brought to them in various foul forms – flies, a bee, a mouse. The children also claimed to have seen the spectral forms of both Amy Denny and Rose Cullender hovering by their bedsides: the ghosts threatened to torture the three girls.

In addition to bewitching the children, the two women were accused of causing a whole list of other misfortunes to their neighbours: the collapse of a cart and the deaths of horses, pigs and cattle.

The Salem witch trial – witnesses collapsing at the witches' approach. The Salem case was influenced by Bury St Edmunds' decisions. (Library of Congress, Prints & Photographs Division, LC-USZ62-475)

They had caused one man to be infested with lice, and they had also caused a chimney to fall down. The final piece of evidence came when Rose Cullender was stripped naked: she was found to have a growth on her body that could only be a teat used to suckle her Devil's familiar (a pig, a cat or a toad).

Both women were found guilty of the charges against them and hanged at Bury's site of execution on Thingoe Hill.

The trial of the Lowestoft witches became notorious and was to have far-reaching repercussions. The presiding judge was Sir Mathew Hale, Lord Chief

Baron of the Exchequer and one of the most eminent and respected judges of his time. The verifying doctor, Sir Thomas Browne, was almost his equal in esteem. The fact that the greatest legal and medical minds of the time had heard the case meant that their judgement and conviction was to set a precedent that would be followed in the future.

In 1692, witchcraft mania reared its ugly head again at Salem in the New England state of Massachusetts. Another wave of witchcraft accusations occurred and the presiding American magistrates could find no

MOYSE'S HALL

For more than 800 years, a solid stone and flint Norman townhouse has occupied the prime north-east corner site overlooking the bustling Buttermarket in Bury St Edmunds. Moyse's Hall has watched over the heart and history of the town, and much of that history is enshrined in the very walls of the building itself. It was possibly the very first stone-built house when everything around it was only timber-framed and in-filled with wattle and daub.

It was probably a merchant's house, with the solid, stone-arched undercroft providing secure storage for goods and merchandise. Later it was probably a tavern, and certainly it passed through periods as a workhouse, a police station and the town jail. In the 1890s, it was briefly used as a fire station, and was threatened with destruction because the fire engines would not fit under the massive arches and between the pillars. Fortunately, common sense (and a national campaign to save this vital part of Bury's heritage) prevailed.

Having witnessed and survived so much, it was almost inevitable that Moyse's Hall would eventually be converted into the town's major museum and, in 1899, it was officially opened in this new role by Lord John Hervey.

There is a display case in Moyse's hall which shows a collection of items used to ward off witchcraft. It includes a mummified cat, witch bottles, and a hoard of shoes that have been discovered at Barley House Farm in Winston. In the seventeenth century, people were afraid of witches creeping into their houses, so they would hide any or all of these strange objects in nooks and crannies, up the chimneys and down the sides of fireplaces, or under doorsteps. These were all the points of entry to a house and it was believed that placing deterrents in these positions would keep the witches out.

All the shoes are very well worn, so it is surmised that when they were worn out the owners just concealed them in the house instead of throwing them away. The idea was that because shoes contain the shape and the strong smell of the people who have worn them, the shape – and especially the smell – would be a protection against witches.

The witch bottles worked on a similar principle. They would have contained human urine or human hair. The witch's familiar was often supposed to be a cat, so it may have been that a dead and mummified cat was buried within the walls would be a bad omen for the witch.

Moyse's hall, at the top of the Buttermarket.

The Saxon Tower.

*The showcase in Moyse's hall containing a
mummified cat and witch bottles.*

and hanged. Two others died in prison, and one man who refused to plead was crushed to death under a board piled high with rocks and stones.

In the aftermath of the English Civil War, 'witch mania' once again reared its ugly head; King Charles had been executed, and the country was in turmoil. It was the perfect background for the fanatical sadist Mathew Hopkins, 'the Witchfinder General', who toured all the Eastern counties torturing confessions from anyone who was unlucky enough to be accused.

His gruesome career lasted for two years, between 1644 and 1646. During that time he is said to have hanged up to 300 witches. In Suffolk alone, over 100 miserable individuals were accused, and at least sixty of them were executed. A boil or any other bump or skin blemish could be pointed out as the witch's supposed 'third nipple', used for feeding his or her Devil's familiar; household cats or a pigs were looked on with particular suspicion.

In Bury St Edmunds forty witches were hanged, eighteen of them in one batch. They included John Lowes, the luckless eighty-year-old vicar of Brandeston church in the Dedham valley. Most victims were old and ugly men and women who had fallen out with their neighbours, but no one was safe.

If no third nipple could be found, then ducking stools could be used to root out witches. The helpless wretches were held underwater for several minutes. Only the drowned were judged innocent.

better guidance on how to proceed than to study the report of the Bury trial of Amy Denny and Rose Cullender, which they read avidly. It provided the perfect model for their response. During the hysteria at Salem, 141 persons – of both sexes – were accused of witchcraft. Again, the accusations were primarily made by two adolescent girls. Of these 122 people were thrown into prison, and nineteen were eventually convicted

MATTHEW HOPKINS.

Matthew Hopkins, the 'Witchfinder General'.

Another divining method, and Hopkins' favourite, was that of pricking with a needle. All witches were said to have at least one spot on their body where they could feel no pain. Consequently the shrieking victims were repeatedly jabbed with a sharp needle in search of a spot which did not make them cry out. Hopkins had a set of silver-handled needles just for this purpose – one of them allegedly with a retractable needle for a painless stab at the accused.

Hopkins was paid up to twenty shillings for each witch he discovered and destroyed, which may have been the real reason for his reign of terror. However, it is perhaps pure poetic justice that Hopkins himself was eventually hanged as a witch: it was claimed that only by being in league with the Devil could Hopkins have successfully rooted out so many witches.

Lowestoft at the time when Amy Denny and Rose Cullender were accused was a small-town community in deep crisis. The town had just suffered a major fire and it was in a serious dispute with neighbouring Great Yarmouth over fishing rights and licences which threatened its future prosperity. In every case it was the old, the helpless and the useless that were primarily attacked and accused. This was not necessarily because they were vulnerable but because, in most cases, they were seen as a burden on the charity of a community which could no longer afford them. Disposing of these people not only provided scapegoats and explanations for the misfortunes all around them, but also got rid of the expense of keeping them.

AD 1604–1836

AFTER THE ABBEY

AFTER THE TERRIBLE shock of the Dissolution, Bury St Edmunds became a quiet country market town in a rural backwater, growing and prospering slowly but steadily with its agricultural base and the wool trade.

Then disaster struck once again: in 1604, the Great Fire of Bury fell upon the town. The blaze started in a malt house in Eastgate Street. It was blamed upon a workman who was accused of letting a fire, lit to dry grain, get out of hand. The flames quickly spread up Northgate Street and into Looms Lane and the Market Place. The inferno lasted for three days, feeding gleefully on the old timber-and-thatch medieval houses. Before the frantic fire-fighting efforts finally brought it to a halt, it had consumed the original Market Cross and the market toll house. When the final count was made, it was estimated that 160 dwellings and more than 500 assorted outhouses had been destroyed. One of the few buildings to

survive in the devastated area was the old merchant's house of Moyse's Hall, which was built of stone.

There were no more major battles in Suffolk, but violent disturbances nonetheless continued. The first major round of rioting after the demise of the Abbey was probably the Maypole riots of 1647. The Puritans were predominant in Bury, and had decided that joy and celebration were definitely sinful. Even Christmas had been banned, and if the festivities surrounding the Birth of Christ were offensive then the Pagan ceremony of dancing in the May was even more of a cause for horror. The erection of a maypole was banned. The ordinary townspeople of Bury said 'stuff that' – or whatever the medieval equivalent was – and up went the Maypole in the Market Square. The outraged town elders ordered it taken down. Rioting promptly began, and the new Roundhead Model Army had to be called in to restore order when the rioters stormed the town magazine.

The west view of the Abbey in the late eighteenth century.

The Great Plague hit London in 1665, and although the disease did not reach Bury, the fear of it caused some complications: three of the aldermen refused to take up their posts because it would mean that they wouldn't be able to flee if the plague did arrive.

More riots followed when James II tried to foist Catholic MPs on the area. When Bury celebrated that King being forced to flee to the Continent in the Glorious Revolution, the town's Catholic mayor was accused of trying to blow up the guildhall; the houses of several other Catholic councillors were ransacked. For good measure, the mob also burned down a new Jesuit college that had only recently been built on the site of the old Abbey ruins.

The 300-year period between 1550 and 1850 has been called the Little Ice Age. It was a time of bitter Siberian winters when Arctic winds must have been blowing down from the north.

In the middle of the freeze, around 1792, just for a change from the usual round of plague and smallpox that kept child death rates high and life expectancy low, Bury was terrorised by a pack of mad dogs and eleven people died from rabies.

By 1816, the cost of the Napoleonic wars had impoverished the whole country, and Suffolk especially was said to be in a very depressed state. In Bury St Edmunds in 1836, the Guildhall feoffees, the aldermen or councillors who ran the town, were busily completing a series of land enclosures which obviously didn't help to ease the sense of public discontent. There was trouble in the surrounding countryside which prompted the Bury magistrates to issue a proclamation saying that they intended to enforce the law against disorderly assemblies and outrages.

This was probably the red rag to the bull, for almost immediately a mob

The Buttermarket, where rioters once gathered.

gathered on the Market Square. The mob then demonstrated its collective displeasure by setting fire to a number of barns in Southgate Street.

The following day an even larger crowd had gathered in the Buttermarket to demand that one Mr Wales, a hosier of Abbeygate Street, should give up his spinning machines. Like the Luddites further north, the labourers of Bury were provoked by the fear that the wave of newly invented machines would take away their jobs. In Suffolk it was agricultural machines that were the main cause for concern,

but a machine was a machine, so for a town mob the hosier's new spinning machines were a fair target. As the mob was getting out of hand, the town magistrates and militia turned out in force to put down the disturbance before they could set fire to anything else.

There was a post-war slump in agricultural prices which left almost a third of Suffolk's working population unemployed. The slump had left farmers without enough money to pay their bills, so tradesmen were also affected. High shop prices were attacked everywhere, and in nearby Brandon 1,500 armed men are said to have wrecked a butcher's shop demanding 'blood or bread.' Perhaps they were confused, and in the heat of the moment mistook the butcher for a baker.

The introduction of mechanisation at this time of economic slump and general unrest was an unhappy coincidence. The general fury of threats and violent upheavals that followed became known as the Swing Riots. All over the county, intimidating notes were left nailed to farm gates. These scrawled notes offered dire threats to terrify the offending farmer into giving up their new threshing or sowing machines for fear of reprisals. Hay stacks and barns were easy enough to burn, so the threat was a real one.

Someone had the bright idea of making it look as though this was a unified campaign with a single mastermind behind it, and all of the notes were signed with the name Captain Swing.

All of this caused the Bury magistrates to swear in extra constables, in an effort to keep the pot from boiling over. They arrested around thirty people for various charges of rioting and machine breaking. Seven of these were transported in a prison ship to Australia for smashing a threshing machine at Withersfield. The constables also managed to apprehend one man for leaving a threatening letter on a farm gate at Stradishall. His name was not Swing, he was not a captain, and it is doubtful if a real Captain Swing ever existed.

The last ripples of turmoil had barely settled before there was a new round of what the magistrates liked to call 'disorderly assemblies and outrages'. This was sparked by calls for voting reform. The existing electoral system for representation at Parliament allowed about thirty selected people to vote for a choice of often only two candidates. The reformers pointed out that such a small number of electors could easily be bribed, and that candidates were often returned to Parliament without the bother of an election.

Obviously, the select few who already held the reins of power had no inclination for any sort of reform. However, popular public opinion was all in favour. The reformers believed that more people should be allowed to vote, at least enough to make bribery expensive, if not impossible. In true Bury tradition, the mob gathered. The Duke of Wellington had become a very popular figure after defeating Napoleon and the French at Waterloo, but now Wellington was a leading opponent against reform. The mob promptly burned his effigy on a huge bonfire at Hog Hill.

They lit another bonfire the following night with the addition of fireworks. If the tradition of November the Fifth had not already been well established it might have caught on, and today we might be burning an annual effigy of Wellington instead of Guy Fawkes.

Another major mob gathering occurred in 1828, when the town elders decided to move the location of the cattle market from its shared location on the Buttermarket to its new home in St Andrews Street, on what was then the outskirts of the town.

THE CATTLE MARKET

———⊘⊘⊘———

Bury St Edmunds has been a thriving market town since before the Norman Conquest of 1066.

Old records show that the market was originally held in what is now St Mary's Square, described as the Horse Market or the Eld, meaning old market. It is not hard to picture the medieval scene, with hogs squealing, cattle and sheep milling in the mud of crude, wood-railed stalls, peasant farmers shouting, gypsies cursing, and soldiers or bailiffs struggling to keep order. The scene would have been overlooked by a few lofty nobles on horse-back, the sacrist, the clerk of the great Abbey, and a few attendant monks keeping a careful eye on their tolls and stall rents.

The original market day was Sunday, but this was changed in 1201 when a visiting Prior preached strongly against the sin of Sunday trading. The Abbot of St Edmundsbury took notice and Tuesday then became the favoured market day. The present market days of Wednesday and Saturday were not fixed until sometime later in the fifteenth century. This doubling of the number of weekly market days points to the growing size and prosperity of Bury St Edmunds in the Middle Ages.

Sometime after the Conquest the market was moved to the Buttermarket, which in those days was literally a market where farmers sold their butter. There was a fish market there too, a corn market and the livestock market. Finally the market outgrew itself — and the town centre — and had to be divided. The noisy, reeking beast market was separated from the conventional market of stalls and traders which remained on the old Buttermarket site, and in 1828 was moved to its new home in St Andrews Street.

At the turn of the nineteenth century, farmers and their families came to market by pony and cart, and sheep, pigs and cattle were driven along the roads in flocks and herds. Turkeys had their feet tarred and sanded to enable them to be driven the long miles from farm to market. The catchment area for a market before the coming of motorised transport was about 7 or 8 miles, for a farmer still had to feed and water his remaining stock before setting off for the market, and he needed to be back the same night. With the coming of the railways some stock could be moved by goods wagon from other major towns, but the flocks and herds still had to be driven on the hoof to and from the railway station.

———⊘⊘⊘———

OPPOSITE *The last days of Bury Cattle Market, which finally closed in 1998.*

Interference with the market was never a wise or popular move. The weekly market had always been an important factor in the lives of farmers and their families, not only in how it affected their livelihood but also as the main social venue of the farming communities. It was a place for doing business and meeting friends, and those who tampered with it were sure to raise strong feelings. A large petition was signed protesting against the change, but it was ignored. Feelings were high and the first market on the new site turned into the almost inevitable riot when an inebriated farmer from Ixworth Thorpe hurled a brick at the town clerk.

The Chartist movement of 1836 was another product of economic depression. It took its name from the People's Charter, which demanded more electoral reforms in the shape of male suffrage, a secret ballot and various other measures. When it was initially rejected it led to great disappointment and another wave of unrest. Around Bury this took shape in a wave of deliberately set rural fires. Haystacks burned. Red glows and black smoke columns filled the skylines. Arson had become a political weapon.

Elections became a good excuse for future protests or celebrations, but gradually Bury became more sedate as

it moved through the genteel and fashionable Georgian era and into the prim and orderly Victorian age. As a social and agricultural centre, the town expanded with many elegant new buildings.

The coming of the railways brought an end to a brief era of mail coaches and the accompaniment of flamboyant highwaymen and footpads who frequently dangled from the local gallows.

In the early days the novelty and excitement aroused by this new, steam-belching form of transport caused two railway workers to opt for an impromptu ride seated on the top of one of the carriages. They had their backs to the engine and sailed happily along until they encountered a low bridge near Thurston. It would have suited the lurid and bloody theme of this book if their heads had been knocked off, but it didn't quite happen that way. However, they did manage to dislodge quite few bricks from the bridge arch and sadly both of the joy riders were killed.

Through all of this, the wealth of the land had shifted. Throughout England, lords and dukes and a new breed of rich London lawyers, bankers and merchants founded great estates with handsome houses on what had previously been Church land; these were to eventually grow into stately halls.

These men courted royalty by hosting great game shoots on their lands, rearing vast flocks of pheasants for the sole purpose of being blasted out of the sky by shot-gun toting sportsmen in their baggy tweeds and deer-stalker hats. The abundance of game birds on the estate lands inevitably attracted the attention of poachers. The ensuing battles of wits between poachers and game-keepers frequently turned to violence, with outbreaks of shooting, cudgelling and fisticuffs. One memorable battle on the Duke of Grafton's estate involved five game-keepers and five poachers. It was an even fight but the poachers lost.

The rich country gentry gradually filled most of the political and higher social roles that had once been the province of the great Abbey, but – like many of the not-so-pious monks and Priors before them – they too had more than few black sheep in their ranks.

AD 1665

THE BLACK SHEEP OF ICKWORTH

THE ESTATE WE now know as Ickworth Park was held by the monks of St Edmundsbury until the reign of Henry VI. Then it was granted to a tenant named William Drury. William's daughter Jane married Thomas Hervey of Thurleigh in Bedfordshire and so began the long history of the Hervey family, who were to become the Earls and later the Marquesses of Bristol.

Despite the West Country title, they retained the family home in Suffolk, and became prominent in local and national politics with a controlling interest in the Borough of Bury St Edmunds. The Herveys were a noble lineage of excellent achievements – but racked with scandal and studded with more than a few black sheep.

Lord John Hervey, the 1st Earl of Bristol, who lived from 1665 to 1754, was a man credited with a great love for the Ickworth estate. He demolished the old manor house which was falling down and moved his family home into one of the farmhouses on the estate. He never achieved his grand plan of rebuilding the manor house but he did plant countless trees and build the summer house and the walled gardens that now grace the park. He also dug out the canal and generally enhanced the overall beauty of the landscape.

He also found time to father twenty-three children with his two wives. Sadly, this was a time when infant mortality was high, even for the nobility and gentry, and four of his children were stillborn; four others only lived for a few days or weeks.

However, his first son by his second wife, the second Lord John Hervey, became the most notorious and controversial of all the Hervey line.

This John Hervey, despite being married and fathering an equally impressive line of children, was bisexual. He made no secret of his male lovers, dressed flamboyantly and rouged his cheeks. In the language of the day, he was a fop and a dandy,

The lake with the summerhouse, the hall, and the family church where the male line of the Herveys are interned.

a man who could 'trip like a lady,' or 'strut like a lord'.

His behaviour in fashionable London society earned him the irreverent title of 'Lord Fanny.' In the eighteenth-century reign of George II, noblemen commonly wore silks and satins, stockings and elaborately curled, powdered and perfumed wigs, but even with this almost effeminate dress code the second Lord John Hervey was flamboyant.

A combination of his camp antics, and a political quarrel with the Earl of Bath, provoked the latter to write a libellous political pamphlet which openly accused Lord Hervey of being a homosexual. This could not go unanswered and the Lord was no coward. He issued a challenge to a duel, although this was equally a crime by law.

They met in St James's Park, where they stripped off their cloaks and crossed swords. Hervey carried in his pocket a letter to the King explaining that he had instigated the duel (thus exonerating his opponent should the other succeed in killing him). He was, after all, still a gentleman.

CULFORD HALL

Ickworth's neighbouring stately hall is in one of five villages which once formed a vast estate, an area which covered over 9,000 acres and existed for nearly 400 years, almost into living memory. Now much of it has been sold to the Forestry Commission and has become part of the King's Forest.

The driveway is entered by a pair of magnificent wrought-iron gates, and if you pass through these you will come to the charming little pebble flint church of St Mary, which was once the estate church. It is framed in splendid old pines and yew trees. Just a little further round the drive is the hall, a huge, stone-faced edifice with a central green cupola, which in its heyday hosted royal shooting parties.

Originally built in 1586 for Sir Nicholas Bacon, the hall was later rebuilt in 1792 for the Marquis of Cornwallis, whose military career took him far away from Suffolk. He was the Lieutenant General in command of the British force at Yorktown in Virginia in 1781. With just over 7,000 men, and outnumbered by more than two to one by the surrounding Americans and French, he was forced to surrender the town to General George Washington, thus bringing to an end the American War of Independence.

Culford Hall has seen many royal visitors – including King Charles II, who caused its closure for ten years or more with a right royal scandal when a rector's daughter, whom he had enticed to his bedroom, threw herself to her death from his upstairs window.

Culford Hall.

Magnificent Ickworth Hall.

The great cupola of Ickworth Hall.

In the event they each managed to inflict a few cuts before they closed in earnest. At that point their seconds intervened by mutual consent and removed their swords. Honour had been duly satisfied.

Three of John Hervey's sons succeeded their grandfather as the 2nd, 3rd and 4th Earls of Bristol. George William was the 2nd Earl until he died in 1775. Augustus John followed him as the 3rd Earl, until his death in 1779; his brother Frederick became the 4th Earl. Frederick was already the Bishop of Derry in Northern Ireland. The position had nothing to do with any great religious faith or sense of calling; like any other position in the upper-class society of the times, it was awarded through political influence. Before his death George had also been Lord Lieutenant of Ireland.

It seems that Frederick had started out well, taking his ecclesiastical duties with some seriousness, but on becoming the Earl-Bishop his interest in Ireland waned. He spent most of his time in his carriage rolling around Europe. He was twice presented to the Pope, but his main interest was in amassing a priceless hoard of European art at his new stately home in Suffolk. The great hall was virtually a museum built to house his stupendous collections.

The Earl-Bishop was a madcap eccentric. He was described by one contemporary as, 'vain, impetuous and delighting in display, an irresponsible adventurer with an insatiable appetite for popularity.' He was also denounced at one stage by King George III as that 'wicked prelate'. Eventually he managed to get himself arrested in Italy on charges of being a spy. Napoleon Bonaparte had emerged in the aftermath of the French Revolution and was busy expanding the glory of France by winning victories over England's allies, including invading Italy. It was a dangerous time to be travelling in Europe and Frederick was on the road from Venice to Rome when he fell ill and was arrested on his sickbed.

It is unclear whether he was a secret agent acting for the British government or merely racing to ransom his latest haul of treasures in order to get them back to England. Either way, he was imprisoned for nine months in the Castello Sforzesco. When he was released he stayed in Italy and there he died on another road from Albano to Rome in July 1803. The crew of the English man-of-war which carried him home objected to having a corpse on board, and so the Earl-Bishop's coffin was concealed in a packing case and labelled as an antique statue.

The scandalising bisexual tendencies of the Hervey family shone through again with Lady Elizabeth, the Earl-Bishop's promiscuous second daughter. She established herself as part of an infamous *ménage a trois* with the Duke and Duchess of Devonshire at their ancestral home of Chatsworth House. She carried on her passionate love affairs with both of them until the Duchess died. Elizabeth then married the Duke and eventually became Duchess in her turn.

The next three generations of Herveys seemed to generally avoid any more serious scandal. Then Victor Frederick Hervey became the 6th Marquis of Bristol in 1960. By then he had already established a wild and free-wheeling reputation as a Mayfair playboy with criminal links in the twilight world of London's Soho. He was bankrupt at twenty-one due to his inept gun-running operations during the course of the Spanish Civil War. Apparently he had tried to double cross the Republicans by betraying a shipment of weapons they had already paid for to the Francoists.

Later, his unsavoury connections with London's underworld led him into the dock of the Old Bailey to face charges of burglary. He had broken into a Mayfair flat and stolen over £2,000 worth of jewellery. He was sent to prison for three years. Victor's defence was that the failure of his latest gun-running enterprise in China had forced him to become a jewel thief.

Despite all of this, the Hervey's have left a magnificent legacy that is now owned by the National Trust.

Hengrave Hall.

THE GREAT ESTATES

Bury was the focal point for a whole circle of great country estates and houses. Some of them have already disappeared. Rushbrooke Hall and Great Barton Hall were both destroyed by fire.

Rushbrooke Hall was built by the prominent Jermyn family in the 1500s. It had a variety of owners – including, for a short time, the Herveys at Ickworth. During the Second World War it became a Red Cross convalescent home for wounded servicemen. After the war it was partially demolished before a major fire broke out and it was totally destroyed.

Great Barton Hall was the home of Sir George Edward Bunbury, who built most of the village of Great Barton and gave his name to its pub, the Bunbury Arms. Another inferno consumed the hall in January of 1914.

Rougham Hall was built around 1690. It was taken over by the British Army during the Second World War. Its wartime role, or its proximity to Rougham airfield, caused it to be hit by a 2,000lb German bomb which exploded in the courtyard. The entire structure was left in ruins; these have now been almost entirely re-claimed by nature, with strangling ivy and encroaching trees.

Two survivors are Euston Hall and Hengrave Hall. Euston Hall is an ancient family home built in the French style, in the 1660s, by the Secretary of State to King Charles II, who was lavishly entertained here in 1671. Later Euston Hall became home to eleven generations of the Dukes of Grafton. The house was re-modeled in the 1750s.

Hengrave Hall is a turreted Tudor mansion which also stands just outside Bury St Edmunds. It has a magnificent oriel window that overhangs the main entrance. This has recently been restored to all its original glory, and the immediate effect is breathtaking. Chubby pink cherubs support the great triple-bay window. The centrepiece above them comprises a golden lion and a red dragon on either side of a quartered shield. On their left is a pair of black unicorns, and to the right a pair of scarlet griffins, again bearing shields.

The most prominent motif that occurs on most of the shields is that of three silver fish on a black background: the device was adopted by Sir Thomas Kytson, who built the hall between 1525 and 1538, after the Abbot of Bury St Edmunds granted him certain fishing rights in the River Lark.

Today Ickworth House is an Italianite marvel with its immense rotunda soaring high above the elegant, palatial wings curving away on either side.

Nearby is the private family church of St Mary. Almost all the male line of the extraordinary Bristol family from the last six centuries is buried here, either in the vault under the church or in the outer churchyard.

The family line has been described as both flawed and gifted, and the finest Palladian mansion in all of Suffolk is both their tombstone and their epitaph.

AD 1878–1945

BURY AT WAR

THE GIBRALTAR BARRACKS is a solid, red-brick two-tower keep which stands on Risbygate Street, at the junction with Westley Road. It is now a military museum, but it was built in 1878 as the Suffolk Regiment's depot and headquarters. The regimental history spans more than three centuries, from 1685, when it was first formed, until 1959, when it was amalgamated into the Royal Anglian Regiment. For nearly 300 years, Bury St Edmunds has been the hub of Suffolk's contribution to every battle for empire and survival.

Like the spokes from a wheel, the Suffolk Regiment's campaigns have radiated out to every corner of the globe. The Suffolk Redcoats have fought in Europe, in Egypt, in India, in Afghanistan and South Africa. They were there at the Somme and at Passchendaele, and at Gallipoli. They were evacuated from Dunkirk and they were back again for the Normandy landings. The long list of their battle honours covers almost every fight for King and Country.

Their main memorial in Bury St Edmunds is the keep itself, and now an additional regimental gallery in Moyse's Hall. However, in the centre of the Buttermarket, half hidden twice a week in the centre of the market stalls, stands the Boer War Memorial, erected in 1904. On top is a weary soldier half rising from a seated position, his rifle gripped ready in his right hand.

The 1st Battalion of the Suffolk Regiment suffered heavy casualties in their first major battle of the Boer War, including the loss of their commanding officer. They had stormed a well-defended hill at Colesberg in South Africa with their Lee Enfield rifles. It was only the beginning of three years of arduous fighting, suffering in their heavy khaki uniforms and cork helmets under a scorching foreign sun. It was standard duty for the Suffolk soldiers, but their courage so impressed the Boers that they renamed the battle

The 12th foot 'Redcoat', the private soldier of 1685 when the Suffolk Regiment was first formed.

The Boer War Memorial in Bury's Buttermarket.

ROUGHAM AIRFIELD

⸺ ❦ ⸺

Rougham Airfield is one of the many East Anglian airfields from which the Mighty Eighth US Air Force flew during the Second World War. It was built on the flat Suffolk farm fields just outside Bury in 1942. It was briefly occupied by the 322nd Bomb Group with their B-26 Marauders. These were later replaced by the 94th Bomb Group with their famous B-17s, the revolutionary Flying Fortress, the first all-metal, four-engine monoplane with its bristling gun turrets.

Those were the days when the sight of the planes and the sound of their engines continuously filled the skies over Suffolk. The 94th flew 324 missions over enemy-occupied Europe. They roared out in defiant close formations, and limped home in smaller, fragmented groups, some of them trailing smoke, many of them never reappearing at all.

Now it has all changed. The few remaining hangars and buildings are part of a small modern industrial estate. The old control tower still stands as a restored museum of aviation history. Half a dozen times each year the skies above will again be filled with aircraft, but these are light, classic biplanes and monoplanes at play, and not the old heavy bombers at war. Rougham has become East Anglia's number-one venue for nostalgic air shows.

⸺ ❦ ⸺

site 'Suffolk Hill,' and built their own memorial on the spot.

However, their finest moments were not always in the heat of battle, for even in the face of disaster the courage and discipline of the Suffolk soldier stood firm. When HMS *Birkenhead* was shipwrecked off the Cape coast in 1852, she carried a draft of seventy privates and one sergeant on their way to fight in the Zulu Wars in South Africa. The men stood by while the women and children were given the scarce places in the lifeboats. Most of these gallant men drowned when the ship went down. A marble role of honour commemorates this event in the Regimental chapel in St Mary's church in Bury St Edmunds, and the order of the day – 'Women and children first' – has gone down in history.

Another reminder of Suffolk courage and regimental glory is the Minden Rose pub, which stands beside the traffic lights on Out Risbygate Street. On 1 August 1759, during the Seven Years War (when Britain was at war with France), the Suffolk Regiment was at the Battle of Minden in Germany. They were among the six British regiments that advanced through murderous cannon fire from concealed enemy artillery, breaking six French cavalry charges that failed to turn them back, and finally winning one of the most splendid infantry victories of any war.

As they advanced, the doughty Suffolk soldiers displayed a flamboyant bravado as they plucked red and yellow roses and wore them jauntily in their hats. Today the Bury pub is named in their honour, and their successors still wear the red and yellow roses on the first of August to commemorate the anniversary of their triumph.

Over the two world wars, the Suffolk soldiers again gave exemplary service. In the First World War, a total of twenty-three battalions of the regiment took part in every major battle, earning eighty-one battle honours. Among over 300 awards for gallantry, two Victoria Crosses were won. The first was won by Sergeant Arthur Frederick Saunders of the 9th Battalion at Loos in September of 1915, and the second by Corporal Sydney James Day at Peronne in 1917.

After his battalion had been forced to retire and his officer had been wounded, Sergeant Saunders won his VC by taking charge of two machine-guns and a handful of men, despite a severe thigh wound which eventually cost him his leg. He closely supported the last four charges of another battalion, and when that battalion was also forced to retire he stuck to his guns, still giving orders and maintaining continuous firing to cover their retirement.

Corporal Day won his award for leading a bombing section detailed to clear a maze of trenches still held by the enemy. In the process he killed two machine-gunners and took four prisoners. When a German stick bomb landed in a trench where there were five other British soldiers, Day grabbed it and threw it back a split second before it exploded. With the trench cleared, he finally established himself in an advanced position and remained, for forty-six hours, at his post under heavy shell, grenade and rifle fire.

In the Second World War, the 1st Battalion of the Suffolk Regiment formed part of the British Expeditionary Force that had to be evacuated at Dunkirk. They fought the rearguard which enabled the main army to withdraw. However, they were back again on 6 June 1944, storming Sword Beach in Normandy as part of the Assault Brigade. This time they were there to stay, fighting their way through France, Belgium, the Netherlands, and then the German heartland, until finally Hitler and his allies were decisively beaten.

The 2nd Battalion was stationed in India at the outbreak of the war, and in November of 1943 they were

GHOSTS BEYOND BURY

⎯⎯ ⊶⊷ ⎯⎯

All of the airfields in the area seem to be haunted by the shades of those who never came back. At Lakenheath it is the story of a phantom hitchhiker in the uniform of an RAF pilot. Apparently, in the spring of 1951 an American military policeman stopped to give him a lift – only to have the ghost simply disappear from his car a few moments later.

⎯⎯ ⊶⊷ ⎯⎯

The memorial to the dead of two world wars on Angel Hill, once bombed by a Zeppelin.

moved into Burma as part of the 'Forgotten' Fourteenth Army. There they fought the Japanese with the utmost skill and bravery, taking a notable part in the Arakan and Imphal campaigns. They, too, fought until the Japanese were finally defeated. Further south, The 4th and 5th Battalions fought equally gallantly in the defence of Singapore, but for once the indomitable Suffolk fighting spirit was not enough. With all her big guns facing the sea, Singapore was never designed to withstand an attack from the Malayan mainland, and was overwhelmed by the sheer weight of numbers of the enemy.

Most of the Suffolk soldiers were taken prisoner and many were forced to work on building the Burma railway, the infamous Railway of Death. Captured, but never defeated, the Suffolk spirit of dignity and determination shone through. Many died, but even as living skeletons many survived. And in those intolerable and inhuman conditions, survival itself was a victory.

For the ordinary people of Bury St Edmunds, their time of testing came when a German Zeppelin of the Luftwaffe appeared in the skies above the town on one bright, moonlit night in 1915, dropping its incendiary bombs and raining down a blaze of merciless machine-gun fire.

The LZ38 was one of Germany's small fleet of airships that had been sporadically bombing London and the coastal towns of England. She was a gigantic grey helium gas balloon 536ft long, powered by four engines and capable of carrying a crew of twenty-two and 2 tons of bombs in the gondola slung underneath.

On this particular night she had already bombed Great Yarmouth and Ipswich before following what was then the A45 further inland. Now it was Bury's turn. The LZ38 still had about forty incendiary and four explosive bombs. She attacked Moreton Hall, apparently without causing any serious damage, and then moved over the town itself. A tree was blown up in Northgate Avenue and a timber yard was hit.

Next the airship swung over the town centre and bombed a house in Angel Hill and then the Buttermarket, setting several shops alight. The Boby Engineering works was attacked – and may have been the main target, as Boby was, at that time, manufacturing munitions for the war effort. Alternatively, the airship may have been simply lost. Early airship navigation was not particularly accurate, and her zigzag route from Yarmouth to Bury suggests she may have been following the patches of bright lights which marked the larger towns.

Theoretically there was a 'no lighting' order in effect, but nobody seemed to be taking much notice. The electric street lights were still on as the airship drifted overhead, and, incredibly, many people switched their house lights on as they were awoken by the noise of the blasts and tried to find out what was happening.

As it returned home, the raiding airship took a wide swing and used the last of its payload to attack the village of Westley. It then dropped a final bomb on the edge of the village of Woolpit, where it left a 500ft diameter crater at Woolpit Warren. Amazingly, despite leaving a trail of havoc, rubble and blazing buildings, no people were killed or injured. The only casualties are said to have been a luckless dog and a few innocent chickens.

The Luftwaffe's airship fleet was small and not particularly reliable. Most of the time they were trying to find their way up the Thames to London and the small biplanes of the Royal Flying Corps generally forced them to fly high where they were out of reach. One airship was shot down over Suffolk near the coast when it lost height, engine and rudder power, and was attacked by three of the tiny RFC fighters. It fell in a ball of flame at Theberton near Leiston.

However, another German airship did find Bury again nearly a year later, on the night of 31 March 1916. A fleet of ten Zeppelins raided Eastern England that night. Among their Suffolk targets, whether planned or by chance, was Sudbury, a munitions factory at Stowmarket, and Bury St Edmunds.

This time the blackout order was being obeyed, but despite this there was severe damage and a death toll of seven. The Buttermarket was attacked again but the main force of the bombing was upon Raingate Street and Springfield road, where several premises were hit and destroyed. More scattered bombs hit other parts of Bury, causing damage and starting fires. If it was a planned attack then the

old Army Barracks in King's Road or the Robert Boby Works may have been the actual targets. Eastgate Station and St Mary's vicarage were both bombed. The station may have been a target but the vicarage was probably just unlucky.

The Zeppelins roamed over East Anglia for several of the following nights but did not return to Bury. It seems that quite often they did not even know which town they were bombing, so their raids were very much hit-or-miss affairs. Overall, the German airships made twenty raids in 1915, peaked at twenty-three in 1916, and then tailed off to seven in 1917 – and only four in 1918, as the war approached its end. Bury was probably lucky in that it was only attacked twice.

During the Second World War, Bury again came under aerial attack. The Zeppelin airships were now obsolete, as the great gas-filled dirigibles had suffered too many a fiery end, but the Luftwaffe now had Dornier and Heinkel bombers – which were much more efficient. In February of 1941, houses in Holderness Road were bombed, killing at least three people and seriously injuring several more. The bombers may have been aiming for the industrial sprawl of the Sugar Beet factory nearby.

The neighbouring town of Newmarket was attacked the same month when a Dornier dropped its bombs along the High Street and destroyed several properties, including the White Hart Hotel. In September, the

AN AMERICAN HERO

Rattlesden Airfield was a close neighbour of Rougham, only a few miles away, and was also opened in 1942 with three massive wartime runways forming a giant triangle. It became the wartime home of the USAF 447th Bomb Group, part of the Mighty Eighth, flying another fleet of thundering B-17s with laconic nicknames like the Squirming Squaw, The Ground Pounder, Rowdy Rebel and Ol' Scrapiron. Between the dark and bloody days from December 1943 and April 1945, they flew 258 combat missions over occupied Europe and Nazi Germany, comprising 8,229 individual flights.

Their initial task was to prepare for the allied invasion of Europe by relentlessly bombing the enemy airfields and missile sites, their naval installations and submarine pens, the great railway marshalling yards, factories and cities and anything that could damage the enemy morale and war effort. After D-Day the motivation shifted to pounding the enemy positions in advance of the beach-heads and aiding the breakout of the allied armies.

A brass plaque beside the door of the old control tower commemorates the heroism of Lieutenant Robert Edward Femoyer of the 711th Bomb squadron, awarded the Medal of Honour for conspicuous gallantry above and beyond the call of duty. Femoyer was killed in action on the 2 Nov 1944. He was severely wounded by anti-aircraft fire over Merseberg Germany but refused pain-killers in order to keep his mind clear to save his plane and his crew. Despite extreme pain and loss of blood he navigated his lone bomber for two and a half hours, clinging to the last slender thread of life until he arrived safely over the English Channel. He died of his wounds shortly after landing.

His was just one of those 8,229 flights, his story just one brief mention from all those now almost forgotten annals of courage and glory.

The plaque commemorating the heroism of Lieutenant Robert Edward Femoyer at Rattlesden airfield.

The B17 Flying Fortress flew in mighty waves from Rougham Airfield.

bombers were back over Bury again and a number of houses were damaged in Fornham Road.

The air raids of the Second World War were no more in number than those of the First World War, probably because German navigation was more precise and they could accurately target London and other large cities. In 1944, the V1 Flying Bombs were hurled at London in Hitler's last-ditch effort at the close of the war, and one of them crashed just to the north of Bury. There was a massive impact and

explosion as the rocket hit the earth, enough to damage a cottage 100 yards away from where it fell.

By the end of the war the whole of East Anglia was virtually one vast aircraft carrier. The RAF bases were hurling up Spitfires and Hurricanes and the lumbering Lancaster bombers. The mighty USAF had arrived in force and filled the rest of the sky with Mustangs and Flying Fortresses. The fighter pilots of the RAF, the gallant few, had pushed the Luftwaffe back over the North Sea – and now it was payback time. The drone of heavy engines filled the Suffolk skies as the combined bomber fleets paved the way for the re-conquest of Europe.

Bury St Edmunds was surrounded by air bases and runways, the nearest being the RAF at Lakenheath and Honington and the Americans at Rougham and Rattlesden. The proximity of so much thundering air traffic eventually brought another disaster.

On the 5 January 1945, two B-17 Flying Fortress bombers of the USAF 490 Bomb Group flew out of their airfield at Eye. Disaster struck, and the two bombers collided in midair and crashed to earth near Bury St Edmunds. On their way down the wreckage hit a USAF P-31 Mustang flying at a lower level to make it a three plane pile-up.

Some of the wreckage crashed into Eastgate Street and one of the engines hit the railway track. The body of one B-17 ploughed into the settling lagoon beside the Sugar Beet factory in Hollow Road. The other crashed at Hall Farm in Fornham St Martin. The ill-fated Mustang crashed near the rugby club south of Bury. Its pilot fell into the grounds of the King Edward VI Grammar School. Altogether seventeen American airmen lost their lives.

There was more to come, for the fires were still smouldering at 8 a.m., when forty-two aircraft of the 94th Bomb Group lined up for takeoff on a mission from Rougham Airfield.

The bombers were airborne with sixty seconds between each take-off but it was a bitter winter's morning with ice everywhere. The B-17, nicknamed 'Mission Mistress', started her take-off at 8.15 a.m., piloted by Lieutenant Jack Collins. She was two-thirds of the way down the runway, past the point of no return, when her number four engine failed. Collins managed to get the plane airborne but with only three engines he could not maintain altitude.

Mission Mistress was carrying a full load of six 1,000lb bombs, plus 2,000 gallons of fuel for the long-scheduled flight into the heart of Germany. Collins jettisoned one of his bombs but it was not enough, and the falling plane crashed at Mount Farm near Moreton Hall on the outskirts of Bury.

The B-17 caught fire on impact and a few minutes later the massive explosions of four of her bombs added to the inferno. The debris scattered for 2.5 miles, and even at that distance the blast blew out doors and windows. Five of her crew died, but four survived.

Another Flying Fortress was to crash at East Barton before the war ended, and Bury received one last visit from the Luftwaffe in March of 1945 when the town was strafed by machine-gun fire.

In August of that year the street lights came on again. Nazi Germany was defeated, and the war in Europe was over.

Other titles published by The History Press

Bloody British History: Liverpool

KEN PYE

This is the LOATHSOME, LURID and DOWNRIGHT LAMENTABLE history of Liverpool! Beginning with the mysteries of the Druids and rushing all the way through to the mud, blood and bullets of the Western Front and the falling bombs of the Blitz, read it if you dare! With more than seventy illustrations (plus a grim and gruesome colour section on the infamous Maybrick poisoning), you'll never look at the city in the same way again!

978 0 7524 6551 7

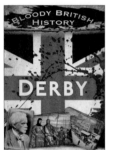

Bloody British History: Derby

PAUL SULLIVAN

This is the real history of Derby – a city built by the Romans over the dead bodies of Britons; burnt by the Vikings; bludgeoned into a Dark Age den of vice by the Saxons; razed once again by the Normans; and simmering with murder, slavery, wickedness and profanity ever since. Featuring the BLACK DEATH, the HORRORS of life in Derby's slums, JACOBITE attacks and OPERATION STARFISH, the incredible plan to foil HITLER'S BOMBERS, you'll never look at the town in the same way again!

978 0 7524 6309 4

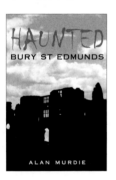

Haunted Bury St Edmunds

ALAN MURDIE

This incredible collection was compiled for The History Press by Alan Murdie, ex-president of the Ghost Club and one of Britain's most respected experts in the field of paranormal research. Filled with extremely rare images and with first-hand accounts of some of the town's – and indeed, the UK's – most terrifying encounters with the supernatural, it will unnerve and amaze visitors and residents alike.

978 0 7524 4204 4

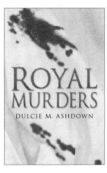

Royal Murders

DULCIE M. ASHDOWN

This book examines the motives, means and consequences of the murders among members of Europe's ruling families over the last 1,000 years. Plucking true stories of historical significance and sheer intrigue, this book tells of violent deaths and royal splendour; tales include the overthrow of tyrants by oppressed populations, murder by witchcraft, and death by knife, bullet and bombs. Take a journey through the dark and tragic side of royal history.

978 0 7524 4937 1

Visit our website and discover thousands of other History Press books.

www.thehistorypress.co.uk

The History Press